PENGUIN BOOKS
MY DAYS IN PRISON

Iftikhar Gilani has been a journalist for the past fourteen years. Having worked for various international and national news agencies and newspapers, he now heads the bureau of the *Kashmir Times* in Delhi. He regularly contributes to Radio Deutsche Welle (Voice of Germany) and is the India correspondent of the Pakistani newspapers *Daily Times*, *Friday Times* and *Khabrain*.

My Days in Prison

IFTIKHAR GILANI

PENGUIN BOOKS

An imprint of Penguin Random House

PENGUIN BOOKS

USA | Canada | UK | Ireland | Australia
New Zealand | India | South Africa | China | Singapore

Penguin Books is part of the Penguin Random House group of companies
whose addresses can be found at global.penguinrandomhouse.com

Published by Penguin Random House India Pvt. Ltd
4th Floor, Capital Tower 1, MG Road,
Gurugram 122 002, Haryana, India

First published by Penguin Books India 2005

Copyright © Iftikhar Gilani 2005
Foreword copyright © Siddharth Varadarajan 2005

All rights reserved

10 9 8 7 6 5 4

ISBN 9780143031550

Typeset in Perpetua by S.R. Enterprises, New Delhi

Printed at Repro India Limited

www.penguin.co.in

This is a legitimate digitally printed version of the book and therefore might not
have certain extra finishing on the cover.

To all those who firmly believe that life and liberty are not the gift of society, state or Constitution but inalienable rights of every individual. The flame of liberty will glow so long as there are persons who have guts, grit and vision to expose and disprove those nibbling away liberty in the name of expedients.

Contents

Foreword

The next time a minister or politician, a policeman or soldier, a bureaucrat, judge or even a journalist tells us he or she cares about the rule of law, I have two words to say: Iftikhar Gilani.

The shocking story that this book tells is not just an indictment of the capriciousness and arbitrariness of power, or a grim chronicle of the sheer viciousness of the Indian state. It is also a depressing account of how all the so-called estates of society—including the Fourth—came face to face with an obvious injustice and were found wanting.

For seven months, Iftikhar—Delhi bureau chief of the Jammu-based daily *Kashmir Times* and a well-respected journalist in the capital—was imprisoned without bail under the draconian and much-abused Official Secrets Act (OSA). His crime: possessing out-of-date information on Indian troop deployments in 'Indian-held Kashmir' culled from a widely circulated monograph published by a Pakistani research institute.

Most readers at this point will think I've made a mistake here. Why would the Indian government invoke the OSA to imprison someone for possessing information put out by Pakistan? The answer is: we really don't know why. Were the intelligence officials who laid the charge stupid? Perhaps. Were they desperate to pin any crime on Iftikhar, no matter how ridiculous? Most likely. Were they confident they could get away with so monstrous a fraud? Almost certainly, for they knew that functionaries and officials in all branches of the state would help them in this task and that their superiors—whose orders they were presumably following—would never allow legal action to be taken against them for malicious prosecution.

Whatever the petty calculations made by the petty men who went after him, we now know from the sequence of events described in this book that for the seven months that Iftikhar grew thin at Tihar Jail, the erstwhile government of Prime Minister Atal Bihari Vajpayee knew he was completely innocent. Yet, the politicians and officials in charge of 'national security' in this country chose deliberately to keep him behind bars.

Taken into custody on 9 June 2002, Iftikhar was finally released on 13 January 2003, after the case against him collapsed under the weight of its own inconsistencies and contradictions. Even this might not have happened but for the ingenuity and persistence of a few journalists who took up Iftikhar's case, ferreted out information that was later to prove useful in demolishing the prosecution case, and kept the continuing scandal of his incarceration and mistreatment a live issue by circulating petitions and badgering ministers and editors at frequent intervals.

Iftikhar is today a free man but, unfortunately, none of the issues that his arrest and incarceration raised have been addressed. More than anything else, his case demonstrated the legal and administrative power of the government's 'national security' apparatus to frame an innocent citizen. Those powers remain untrammelled. The OSA is bad enough, but if one considers the fact that the same system which framed Iftikhar under it also has laws like the Prevention of Terrorism Act (or its new avatar, the Unlawful Activities Prevention Act) at its disposal, the possibilities for misuse are almost limitless.

We now know that the initial decision to arrest Iftikhar was not the result of the serendipitous discovery of a file on his computer that aroused suspicion. The IB officials who trawled his hard drive came across a file with the heading 'Fact Sheet on Indian Forces in Indian-Held Kashmir'. Sensing that they had finally found something potentially useful, the officials manually replaced all references to Indian-held Kashmir—a Pakistani term used to refer to those parts of Jammu and Kashmir not under their control—with the words 'Jammu and Kashmir', to suggest the file was extracted from an official Indian document. They then added the words 'Only for Reference. Strictly not for publication or circulation', to heighten the suggestion of secrecy.

The first sin was committed at this point, when the IB fabricated evidence. But there was much more to come. The Directorate General of Military Intelligence (DGMI), which was tasked with evaluating the significance of the IB's find, refused to pronounce a verdict of its own. Since it had been given a photocopy of the original Pakistani monograph, it could not but have known that there was no case and that Iftikhar was innocent. Indeed, this was precisely the opinion it rendered when, six months later, it was asked to re-evaluate the evidence against the journalist. But in June, for reasons that need to be probed, the DGMI and its hierarchy allowed themselves to be party to the rendering of an opinion (the information recovered could be 'directly useful to our adversary') that they knew to be false.

Since the DGMI 'opinion' made no reference to the published document, Iftikhar's counsel tried in vain to have the courts take cognisance of it and demand that the military provide a second opinion expeditiously. Here, the case hit its third and fourth roadblocks, which was the timorousness of the lower judiciary and media in matters ostensibly relating to national security and official secrets. What was surprising was that despite the alacrity of the courts in filing contempt proceedings against those who try to manipulate the course of justice by misreporting or misrepresenting what transpires during a hearing, the concerned judge took no action against a wholly fabricated news report which appeared in a national daily the first time Iftikhar was produced in court: 'In the course of hearing on Monday, Geelani [sic] reportedly said he had been passing on classified information about the movement of Indian troops to the ISI. When chief metropolitan magistrate Sangita Sehgal asked him if she should record this in his statement, Geelani nodded in assent.'[1]

The news was false and amounted to contempt of court. Yet, no action was taken.

As for the gullible newspaper's crime reporter who was fed this story by the Delhi Police Special Cell, she never made a personal apology, though the newspaper later made amends and published a denial. I happened to be introduced to the reporter in question at a colleague's wedding in 2004 and when I said I had a bone to pick with her because of the hit-job she had done on Iftikhar Gilani, she said, 'I don't know any Iftikhar Gilani.' I was angry but decided to give her a bit of advice: 'The police officials who used you to plant that story have escaped with their reputations intact. But what you did will remain a blot on your reputation as a journalist so long as you don t apologize to Iftikhar.'

Neeta Sharma's story was important to the police because it appeared just at a time when a petition drafted by Aunohita

---

[1] Neeta Sharma, 'Iftikar Geelani admits ISI links', *Hindustan Times*, 11 June 2002

Mojumdar and other journalists and friends of Iftikhar was gathering steam. A brief report about the campaign had appeared in the *Times of India* on 10 June and the police and the Intelligence Bureau (IB) quickly realized the need to nip any journalistic acts of solidarity in the bud. Editors could be leaned upon (and they were) but there was no better deterrent to the campaigning spirit than a concocted confession by Iftikhar that he had been an ISI agent all along. Soon, the floodgates opened and any number of malicious reports appeared across much of the Indian media accusing Iftikhar of being a traitor and militant, smuggler and jihadi, a sex fiend and 'spy claiming the privileges of a newsman', in the libellous words of the Bharatiya Janata Party MP and one-time journalist, Balbir K. Punj.[2]

But if journalists erred in straying from the path of professionalism, theirs was a minor transgression compared to the moral and legal callisthenics of the ministry of home affairs (MHA) officials. When the DGMI's second opinion, delivered in December 2002, absolved Iftikhar of any wrong doing, the ministry decided it would not be deterred from its 'nationalist' duty of keeping an innocent journalist imprisoned at any cost. The Union law ministry was consulted and at a high-level meeting chaired by as senior an official as Special Secretary (Jammu and Kashmir affairs) A.K. Bhandari on 26 December 2002, the decision was taken to dismiss the DGMI's inconvenient opinion as 'irrelevant'. Even though military intelligence was now conceding that the information recovered from Iftikhar's computer had been compiled in Pakistan, the MHA felt the same was 'prejudicial to the safety and security of the country' and that Iftikhar had to be prosecuted. On 7 January 2003, this was indeed the stand the MHA took in court.

---

[2] Balbir K. Punj, 'Dissimulation in words and in images', *Outlook*, 8 July 2002

Puzzled by the MHA's stand, I spoke with a very senior official in the ministry later that day. 'You people say Gilani had a published document,' he said, justifying the case. 'But you forget it has been published in Pakistan.' And how does that make it illegal, I asked. In any case, the Institute for Defence Studies and Analyses library in Delhi also has a copy of this document, I said. 'Are you sure of it?' he shot back. The Kafkaesque conversation ended with the official promising to disclose yet more details about Iftikhar's treasonable document collection at a subsequent date. Before that date, however, the home ministry developed cold feet. Faced with the prospect of a showdown in court between the MHA and DGMI, someone somewhere decided discretion was the better part of valour. Without so much as a word of explanation or apology, the case was quietly withdrawn 'for administrative reasons and in the public interest'.

Strangely, the official I mentioned in the preceding paragraph was not done. He rang me up the day after Iftikhar was released to complain about the critical tone of an opinion piece I had written on the subject. 'Do you know, there are a lot of other things he has done which you don't know about,' he told me. Such as what, I asked. 'You know he had five or six visa forms for Pakistan?' The conversation was clearly not going anywhere and we agreed to discuss the matter later. I put down the phone, opened my own drawer and counted three Pakistani visa forms. If six forms netted Iftikhar seven months in Tihar, how many was I going to get for three? Fortunately for our civil liberties, that official has since retired and left the MHA. Less fortunately, however, he is now helping to run an equally important government organization.

Iftikhar is a gentle, modest man who has put up with great pain and humiliation and come through a terrible ordeal with his dignity and honour intact. He has told his story here with the honesty and integrity that are the hallmarks of his craft as a journalist. There is also pathos and black humour in abundant measure. Most importantly, Iftikhar has used his skills as a journalist to transcend the immediacy and specificity of his own case and focus attention on the plight of the system's other victims. The story he tells here is not just his own but also of those other unfortunate souls charged under the OSA in what seem like trumped up cases. Of those who are tortured and beaten in our prisons. Of those who fall foul of the sadistic, dehumanizing ways of jail officials.

Iftikhar does not say so but it seems to me unacceptable that he should have been through the ordeal he has without someone in the system—politician, policeman, sleuth and bureaucrat—having to pay a price for what was an obvious case of malicious prosecution. Apart from monetary compensation, there is urgent need to fix individual criminal responsibility on the part of the concerned officials. Apart from the IB officials named by Iftikhar, who knew the document on his computer had deliberately been tampered with? Who prevailed upon the DGMI to give a bogus opinion on the document the first time around? Who planted false stories in the media? The erstwhile Vajpayee government clearly had no incentive to ask these questions and it is doubtful any other government would want to expose to the public the true nature of how unprofessional and vindictive our law enforcement agencies can be. But the courts are a different matter. I hope every sitting justice of the Supreme Court reads this book. And I would urge the apex court to take suo motu notice of this case and direct the Criminal Bureau of Investigation to prosecute the officials responsible under the relevant provisions of the Indian Penal Code barring malicious legal proceedings. Iftikhar spent nearly seven months in Tihar Jail. I am willing to wager that a month or two there—or even longer—might make law enforcement officials think twice before settling on another innocent victim.

As for the OSA, a colonial era law that has no place in the statute books of a democratic society, it needs to be repealed or drastically amended so as to end all scope for misuse.

1 February 2005   Siddharth Varadarajan

Siddharth Varadarajan is Deputy Editor of the Hindu. *His edited volume on the Gujarat violence,* Gujarat: The Making of a Tragedy, *was published by Penguin in 2002.*

One
Freedom Restored

13 January 2003, 6.00 p.m.

I could not believe that it was not a dream. That I was actually going to be free again. Free from the incarceration, the charges and, hopefully, the stigma.

I was about to be released from Tihar Central Jail No. 3.

I was taken to the deodhi where a durwan, completing the formalities for my release, asked mechanically, 'Your name?'

'Iftikhar Gilani.'

'Father's name? Age? Identification marks?' he continued, his face completely expressionless.

I replied like a schoolboy in the principal's office. After seven months in jail, fear and obedience came instinctively to me.

After he had finished, Superintendent R.P. Meena and his deputy, who were watching the proceedings, bade me goodbye. I was escorted to the giant gate that stood between the secret world of Tihar Jail and the outside world. I had often wondered if that gate would ever open for me. I did not believe it would.

A small wicket gate led me to the outside. For seven long months I had dreamt of this moment. I took a deep, shuddering breath, and then turned around for a final look at the jail. The wicket gate was closed. It was goodbye to a dreadful past.

While I was savouring the fresh air of freedom, I heard someone say, Get into this ambulance, Gilani.' It was an assistant superintendent standing beside the ambulance. There was another officer next to him. The driver was in his seat and the engine was running. Before I knew what was happening, I was pushed into the back of the vehicle, the two officers got in, sat on either side of me, and ordered the driver to move. In the process my knee was grazed quite badly. But that pain was nothing compared to the dread I felt when I noticed that the ambulance was not going towards the main gate meant for the release of prisoners. In spite of the cold I began sweating. All kinds of horrible thoughts stormed my mind. Perhaps my relief had been premature. Perhaps I was going to be rearrested under some other charge, like the many political prisoners in Kashmir whose detentions had been repeatedly extended under one or the other pretext. What if they were planning to kill me in a fake encounter? My hopes of freedom were dying fast. But I could not muster the courage to ask the jail officials where we were going. After all, they were not accustomed to responding to questions of prisoners. Their business was only to command them.

Suddenly two cars, one a Maruti, the other a Santro, appeared behind the ambulance. One of the assistant superintendents panicked and asked the driver to accelerate. The cars too increased their speed. It was clear they were chasing the ambulance. My heart thudded violently as the ambulance moved faster. At the same time, I felt a hollowness in the pit of my stomach. The bumpy road we were driving on inside the jail complex was generally used for transporting bodies of prisoners for a quiet burial or cremation.

Within a few moments the two cars closed in and overtook the ambulance. The man inside the Maruti signalled the ambulance to stop. I was now convinced that something terrible was in store for me again. My scepticism was not unfounded. So many times during my incarceration I had been assured that freedom was just around the corner, that I would be granted bail and released on the next date of hearing. Each time, all I got was an extension of judicial custody.

The ambulance halted near the office of the Director General (Prisons) and it was the personal secretary to the DG (Prisons) who had waved us down. One of the assistant superintendents got out, and spoke to him. The doors of the Santro opened. My friends Jal Khambatta and Umakant Lakhera got out of the car. To say that I heaved a sigh of relief will be an understatement.

The other assistant superintendent joined his colleague outside and together they ascertained the identities of my friends and then verified them against the documents they had with them. One of them asked me whether I knew them.

I replied in the affirmative. I was then told to disembark from the ambulance and board the Santro. Our car took an ordained route behind the car of the personal secretary which led us to the outside world. He said goodbye to us outside the jail complex.

I was going back home. Finally. I did not know what it would look like. Seven months in detention seemed like a lifetime. I had well-nigh forgotten the faces of my children. During my court appearances I remembered seeing only the pale faces of my wife, Aanisa, and a few close friends. The feeling was overwhelming. I was still not able to appreciate fully that I was free. My friends took me and my family to a small party organized by my lawyer V.K. Ohri to celebrate Lohri, which happened to fall on that day. I was very uncomfortable at the party. I would have much preferred to talk to my friends, to share my joy with them, to convince myself that I was really free. That the ordeal was finally over.

■

Until a few days ago I was a dangerous Pakistani spy in the eyes of the government. I was accused of collecting data on army formations and deployment of security forces in Jammu and Kashmir. In fact the Military Intelligence had certified that a document recovered from my computer contained information gathered by 'an agent specifically tasked to do so'. The said document was a detailed ORBAT (Order of Battle) of Army, Rashtriya Rifles and Para Military Forces deployed in Jammu and Kashmir. Therefore I was charged under Section 3 and Section 9 of the Official Secrets Act of 1923 which entailed a fourteen-year jail term. Besides I had been accused of being a sexual pervert and charged under Section 292 of the Indian Penal Code for promotion of pornography.

It had taken seven months of depositions, adjournments and empty promises of bail before the decision to release me was taken. The news that the government had decided to withdraw charges against me and had moved an application before the court of the Chief Metropolitan Magistrate (CMM) was first broken by the Urdu Service of the BBC. On that dull evening of 10 January 2003, locked inside Barracks No. 5 of Ward No.11, a small one-band radio purchased in the jail itself brought the cheerful news of my imminent freedom. My fellow inmates Arvind, Anil and Ahtisham embraced me with tears of joy. There was a growing excitement in my mind, but I kept my composure. In fact I did not utter a single word.

My fellow inmates were puzzled. They could not understand my lack of emotion. People generally broke down, whooped ecstatically, laughed hysterically or danced around when their release was announced over the public address system of the jail. Finally, Gagandeep Singh, a fellow inmate, asked me, 'What has happened to you, Iftikhar—don't you believe the news?'

I did not know what to say to him. Perhaps I had become 'depersonalized' as Dr Viktor E. Frankl describes in his best-seller *Man's Search for Meaning*. The famous European psychiatrist, who had spent years in a Nazi concentration camp, says, 'Psychologically, what was happening to the liberated prisoners could be called "depersonalization". Everything appeared unreal, unlikely, as in a dream. We could not believe it was true. How often in the past years had we been deceived by dreams! We dreamt that the day of liberation had come, that we had been set free, had returned home, greeted our friends, embraced our wives, sat down at the table and started to tell all the things we had gone through—even of how we had often seen the day of liberation in our dreams. And then a whistle shrilled in our ears, the signal to get up and our dreams of freedom came to an end. And now the dream had come true. But could we truly believe in it?'

Countless times during my stay at Tihar my wife and friends told me that I would soon be out, but nothing had happened. So I had stopped thinking about my release. I had seen so many people suffering under the Official Secrets Act for much longer periods. Allegations and supporting evidence against them were even flimsier than what the prosecution had been able to cobble together against me. I had seen many poor people languishing in jail for petty offences. Offences that I did not believe were worthy of arrest and imprisonment. I realized that the law is a perplexing creature and those handling this instrument were themselves quite wily. They knew their craft pretty well. So I had turned rather cynical and become resigned to my fate: a prolonged stay in jail.

The next two days were uneventful except that the news of my imminent release had made me a hero of sorts among the inmates. Many saw a saviour in me. Others saw a ray of hope for themselves. I was virtually flooded with congratulations and good wishes. How was I going to express my gratitude to them? A sense of attachment and duty engulfed me. I knew that many of the inmates were criminals, but a great number of them were in that horrific situation for almost nothing. There was no logical explanation for their predicament except that it was their fate. Some of these people had reconciled to life in jail, some wanted revenge, some justice and many just wanted to get out and piece together their lives afresh. Every one of the prisoners had a tale to tell. Those whose lives had been shattered, whose families were pauperized by some malicious individuals, hoped that I would carry their tales to the outside world. Perhaps some conscientious officer or political leader would understand their plight and do something for them too. I did not know how I would be able fulfil their expectations.

In the meantime, the print and electronic media had reported that the government had decided to withdraw charges against me. Many people mistook me for S.A.R. Geelani, the Delhi University lecturer convicted in the Parliament House attack case. They were quite indignant that the government was withdrawing charges against someone whom the courts had pronounced guilty just a few days ago. How could I convince them that I was only an innocent journalist doing my job and not a hard core spy? Would they believe me?

TWO
They Had Come for Me

Just as my release from prison was unexpected and full of drama, so was my arrest and remand to judicial and then police custody. It all started on Sunday, 9 June 2002.

My work schedule had been quite hectic and I had not been able to take even one Sunday off for the past four weeks. Even the previous night I had worked till 1.00 a.m. preparing my weekly column for the *Friday Times*, Lahore. I had planned to sleep through the morning the following day. Suddenly I was awakened by my wife, Aanisa, mumbling sleepily in Kashmiri, '*Kus tan chhhu darwazes peth.*' (Somebody is at the door.)

Before I could respond there was another loud knock.

I switched on the light.

It was 4.30 a.m.

Wondering whether we had imagined it, since the doorbell had not been rung, or if there really was someone outside, I staggered to the front door. As I reached it, I heard voices.

'It looks like these people have fled the place.'

Half-awake, I opened the door.

Two SLR-toting policemen of the Central Industrial Security Force (CISF) barged inside, their guns trained on me. Ten to twelve persons stood outside.

Everything happened so fast that I was stunned. A smart-looking middle-aged man walked in and introduced himself: 'I am Vikram Sahai from the Income Tax Department. I have the authorization to search your house.'

He showed me a piece of paper. It had my name along with the name of my father-in-law, Syed Ali Shah Geelani, and my address on the top. He asked me to put my signature on it. I could not see what else the paper said, but numbly I signed it.

'Now that you have already entered my house you may as well search it,' I said to him, fully awake by then. I pointed to the armed CISF personnel and asked, 'Why all this paraphernalia? Is there any need to point guns at me? Do you think I am a terrorist?'

Sahai told the policemen to lower their arms.

'You may search my house but for God's sake do not make a tamasha out of me. I have to live in this locality. The presence of these gun-bearing security personnel outside my house will severely harm my reputation. My neighbours may mistake me for a terrorist or a criminal,' I added.

Vikram Sahai asked the raiding party members, which included a woman, standing near the staircase to come inside. They entered the house and, as swiftly as commandos raiding a terrorist hideout, took over every room, including the bedroom where my wife was lying half-awake.

I have a small flat on the first floor of an unauthorized colony in Delhi. It has two bedrooms, a study-cum-office, a kitchen, a drawing room and a small lobby-cum-dining-area. The drawing room and the study look out on an open space in the colony. The lobby lies between these two rooms and the bedrooms and the kitchen. The main door opens into the lobby while a side door for guests leads into the drawing room, in keeping with traditional Kashmiri homes.

A stunned and shaken Aanisa wanted to change out of her nightdress before coming into the drawing room, but the security personnel would not leave the room. So she picked up her clothes and made to enter the bathroom. The lady officer followed her and instructed her not to close the door. My wife was robbed of her privacy. I was furious, and objected to this behaviour, but no one paid heed.

Sahai wanted to know where my phone was. I took him to my study-cum-office. He asked me to leave the room and got on the phone. I went to the lobby. Every room was occupied by Sahai's men. After some twenty minutes Sahai came out.

As a courtesy my wife asked him, 'Would you like some tea?'

'No, there is no need for tea—we are here on work,' he replied.

In spite of that Aanisa prepared tea for all of them, but they didn't touch it. However they allowed us to have it. This was to be the only refreshment we would have for the next eighteen hours. We would not be allowed even a drop of water in the sultry heat of June. But we did not know it at that time.

After his phone conversation Sahai asked me to accompany him to the flat where my father-in-law used to stay while in Delhi. I thought they had come to raid his house and the whole matter pertained to him only. Being a prominent leader of the All Parties' Hurriyat Conference, a conglomerate of twenty-three political groups questioning Jammu and Kashmir's accession to India, he had been subjected to such actions by the government in the past.

Syed Ali Shah Geelani was not in Delhi at that time. I took the keys to his small two-bedroom flat in a nearby building and went out with Sahai. As soon as I stepped into the street, I saw a large number of armed policemen in a battle-ready position, their weapons pointing to my house. I was surprised as I had thought the entire raiding party was inside my flat and the raid was going to be a quiet affair. Their presence had struck terror into the whole locality.

Many more surprises, rather shocks, awaited me.

When we reached the flat, I saw a large crowd outside the building. The flat was already open and around twenty people were sitting inside. The lock was not broken. Apparently, they had the keys. They told me to stay there and answer any questions they asked.

'I do not know anything about this place as I do not come here much. Perhaps my wife will be able to tell you, if she knows, since she visits her father whenever he is here,' I said.

Sahai took me back to my house. He asked me to stay in the lobby and not enter my study-cum-office or the drawing room. He told my wife to accompany one of his men to her father's residence.

It was now around 6.00 a.m.

My wife went to her father's home. The search operation had already started. The whole place had been turned upside down.

While I was out with Sahai, the team in my house had started their 'search operation', though ransacking seemed a more apt term.

Every now and then someone would bring a sheet of paper or a book and question me about it. I would answer and they would go back to my office or the drawing room. By 8.00 a.m. they had completed the search of the whole place except for one wardrobe in the bedroom, the keys to which were with Aanisa. While they waited for her to return, one of them went out and brought breakfast for the team.

All of them huddled together in the office and drawing room and ate their breakfast. I sat by myself in the lobby wondering when they would finish their work.

'Is there water in the fridge?' one of the raiding party asked, opening my refrigerator.

'See if there is,' I told him somewhat belligerently.

I was feeling hungry and wanted to eat but Aanisa was still at her father's place and our kitchen, rather our whole house, was under the control of these uninvited guests.

I could not believe that the same people who had politely refused to have the tea Aanisa had offered them a few hours ago did not have the elementary courtesy of seeking my permission to use my kitchen and refrigerator. I was thinking of etiquette and propriety at the time, but I had no idea then of what lay in store for me and my family. Fortunately, our children aged four and two and a half were not with us then. Their presence would have added to our distress.

In my office, an animated discussion about the operation was in progress. Some were saying that since nothing objectionable had been recovered no action could be taken. Others argued that something had to be done about me as the news had already spread. That was when it struck me that they had designs on me as well. All this while I had thought that they had some information about my father-in-law and were acting upon it. Sitting there, it gradually dawned on me that this was not a simple raid by the Income Tax Department. I wondered if the Income Tax raid was only a cover for the actual raid which was being conducted by the Intelligence Bureau (IB), the central agency tasked with carrying out intelligence activities inside the country.

Around 9.00 a.m. the raiding party finished their breakfast as well as the discussion. Their decision: search the place all over again.

The party got to work. Vikram Sahai sat with me in the lobby. 'Give me your car keys,' he said.

I went to the desk and handed over my bus pass to him.

Sahai looked at the card and then at me, puzzled.

'I do not have a car. I travel by DTC [Delhi Transport Corporation] buses,' I said.

He did not believe me and despatched one of his men to find out from the neighbours. They confirmed that I did not own a car. Then I was asked about my mobile phone. I told them that I did not have one. Next he wanted to know my Internet account password, which I promptly provided.

By now I was able to distinguish, with a fair amount of accuracy, between the officers of the Income Tax Department and those of the IB. The behaviour of the Income Tax officials was markedly polite, while the IB sleuths were high-handed and rude.

Just then a man came to the lobby with my address book in his hand. He was marking on it with a pen. I requested him not to tamper with it.

'Tell that sahib,' he replied, pointing towards a dark-complexioned, thin, tall man standing nearby.

'Hey, do not obstruct official work,' he warned me and told the man to get on with his job.

Sahai asked me to switch on my computer. I obliged. He started scanning the stored data. After about half an hour he shut it down. He did not take any printout.

Soon a few more officials joined the raiding party. All of them were from the IB. I was asked to switch on the computer again by an IB official whose name, I came to know later on, was Majid. He was a fair and medium-built fellow. He scanned my computer and kept on asking me about the contents. In between he took printouts of some of the files. He came across a file named 'Forces'. Casually he asked me about the contents of that file. I told him that it was a download from the Internet meant as background material. He took a printout of this file as well.

At this point, certain incidents which had been puzzling me for several days began to fall in place and I was able to make sense of them.

For the last two days, that is from 7 June 2002, I had not been receiving any e-mails. Since my e-mail is an official one of the Delhi Bureau of the *Kashmir Times* and is published every day in the printline, I receive more than a hundred e-mails every day. Yes, my e-mail account had been blocked. I had complained to the service provider, VSNL, that my stories were neither reaching the destination nor were they bouncing back. But VSNL could not offer a satisfactory reply.

I also learned later from my neighbours that for several days before that fateful morning, a Maruti car with three or four people used to be parked in the vicinity of my flat throughout the day. One neighbour had even questioned their credentials. They had firmly told him to mind his own business as they were from the police.

Around 10.30 a.m. there was a sort of panic among the raiding party. More IB sleuths had joined the operation. They hurried to draw the curtains on all the windows facing the open space in the colony. I went into the study to see what the matter was. The locality was swarming with camera crews of various news channels. This gave credence to my hunch that the raid was not a bona fide one but meant for propaganda purposes. As I stood there contemplating the situation, an IB officer shouted from the study room, 'Go back inside and do not come here again.'

I went back to the lobby. The study and drawing room remained out of bounds for me for the rest of the day. I politely asked

Sahai why the mediapersons were there. He seemed equally surprised and said that his department had not informed anybody in the media about the raid.

That reminded me of one seemingly innocuous phone call I had received from a journalist friend at around 12.00 the previous night while I was working on the column for the *Friday Times*. He was from the Press Trust of India (PTI) and had called to ask me whether my father-in-law's place was being raided. Not to my knowledge, I told him. The call ended and I forgot about it.

But now it was clear that some journalists had been tipped off about a news scoop they could look forward to. Being a journalist I know that such 'leaks' from interested agencies are quite common.

Most of the CISF men had left the locality by the time the media teams arrived, except for two who were acting as witnesses in the search operation. These two remained for the whole day. I found it strange that the raiding party did not make any effort to get witnesses from our pretty densely populated colony.

More than five hours had elapsed and Aanisa had still not returned from her father's flat. I was worried. I asked Sahai about her. He assured me that there was nothing to worry about—she would be back in a while.

There, Aanisa was made to help the raiding party in deciphering what her father had written in Urdu. She was also asked to read the Urdu books lying around. The lady officer who had accompanied Aanisa was quite overbearing and kept threatening to put her behind bars if she did not cooperate.

By the time Aanisa returned from her father's flat after the search was completed, more officers from the IB had arrived.

There must have been about sixty of them in the house by now. They asked Aanisa to hand them the keys to the wardrobe. They had already rummaged through the whole bedroom. Suitcases lay open and clothes and papers were strewn all around. The wardrobe was also thoroughly searched. One officer sitting in the drawing room asked Aanisa to show them her jewellery. She took out a small pouch from the locker of the wardrobe and gave it to the officer. The officer was surprised. *'Bas itna hi hai?'* he asked incredulously and they all burst out laughing. They made an inventory of the jewellery. After huddling together for some time they returned the jewellery.

During this period my wife and I were subjected to some sort of psychological pressure. The IB officers took turns to ask us the same questions repeatedly. One person would come to where we were sitting and ask one set of questions. After a few minutes another man would come and ask another set of questions. Then a third person would repeat the first set. And so on it went until around 2.00 p.m.

Suddenly, a foreign journalist entered the lobby.

'What has been found—how much cash has been recovered in the search?' he asked. At once some officials pushed him out and shut the door.

'Why don't you show the media what you have found here?' I asked Sahai sarcastically. There was no reply. This was in contrast to the way 'recoveries' from my father-in-law's house in Srinagar were being showcased before the media.

The search operation was suspended for a while. Lunch packets for the team had arrived. All of them had their lunch, ignoring our presence. After they had finished eating they asked Aanisa and me to get into the bedroom and bolted the door from outside. We were confined to that untidy, mindlessly plundered bedroom for five hours. Both of us were exhausted from the tension and anxiety. Neither of us knew what to do. Finally at about 7.00 p.m. the door was opened.

By this time I was convinced that the raid conducted on my residence was actually an IB raid in the garb of an Income Tax raid. For one, the raiding party consisted of a disproportionate number of IB sleuths, who seemed to be in command. The Income Tax officials did try to act according to the law but they were simply overruled by the IB officers. The contrast and tussle between them was clearly visible.

Since the authorization to search my house had come from the Income Tax Department, the search operation was totally illegal, as can be seen from the report of the Tax Reforms Committee headed by Prof. Raja Chelliah. While recommending the presence of a legal consultant during the search, the report said:

> The major focus of the search must be to unearth documents revealing concealed income as well as assets such as money, jewellery and other valuable articles. Section 132 authorizes the search officer to record a statement by any person found in the premises which may be used in evidence before any Court proceedings. Since interrogation is not a part of the object of the search, it must be ensured that the assessee is not interrogated under intimidation and is not coerced into making a confessional statement.

In my case, the raiding party was not looking for any document showing concealment of income or money. Had that been the objective, the search would have ended by 12.30 p.m. as they had not been able to find any document revealing concealed income or money or jewellery. All they had found was a princely sum of 3450 rupees, besides a few gold ornaments. Though this was disclosed later in the charge sheet, the media were led to believe that vast amounts of money and jewellery had been recovered from my flat.

The raiding party members were more curious about the news reports, books and other documents present in my study-cum-office. I also work for Radio Deutsche Welle (Urdu Service). I used to write the reports in Urdu in my own handwriting and read them out over the telephone. One of the policemen knew a little Urdu. When some IB men in the raiding party saw these papers, they asked him to read them, as well as the many Urdu books lying there. The poor man was at sea, what with his limited knowledge and my not too legible long hand! In the end they decided to bundle up most of these reports and take them away for detailed examination. Imagine my horror when Dominique Lapierre's *Freedom at Midnight* was sealed and declared a contraband item! However, after some persuasion they spared Lapierre and E.M. Forster. As per section 132(1)(iii) of the Income Tax Act, only such books of account and other documents can be seized which the assessee has failed to produce in response to notice under section 142(1) or under section 131 or which he will not or would not produce.

Also according to section 132(1) of the Income Tax Act, an Income Tax search can be ordered by a competent Income Tax authority who, in consequence of information in his possession, has reason to believe that:

(a) any person to whom a summons under sub-section (1) of section 37 of the Indian Income-tax Act, 1922 (11 of 1922), or under sub-section (1) of section 131 of this Act, or a notice under sub-section (4) of section 22 of the Indian Income-tax Act, 1922, or under sub-section (1) of section 142 of this Act was issued to produce, or cause to be produced, any books of account or other documents has omitted or failed to produce, or cause to be produced, such books of account or other documents as required by such summons or notice,

(b) any person to whom a summons or notice as aforesaid has been or might be issued will not, or would not, produce or cause to be produced, any books of account or other documents which will be useful for, or relevant to, any proceeding under the Indian Income-tax Act, 1922 (11 of 1922), or under this Act,

(c) any person in possession of any money, bullion, jewellery or other valuable article or thing and such money, bullion, jewellery or other valuable article or thing represents either wholly or partly income or property [which has not been, or would not be, disclosed] for the purposes of the Indian Income-tax Act, 1922 (11 of 1922), or this Act (hereinafter in this section referred to as the undisclosed income or property)…

None of the above conditions necessitating the conduct of a search were present. No summons or notice was issued to me under any provision of the Income Tax Act and there was no reason to believe that I would not produce 'any books of account or other documents' if so required by the Income Tax authorities. The third condition regarding possession of 'undisclosed' income was also absent.

The following were the 'documents and books of account' recovered from my house: Details of the bank accounts held by me and members of my family, registered documents regarding the flat where I was living, one fixed deposit receipt for 10,000 rupees and a certificate of investment in a plantation company of 50,000 rupees made several years ago, payment for which was by a crossed cheque. Therefore the raid on my premises could not be justified under any of the conditions of the Income Tax Act. So I was convinced it was politically motivated. My name and address had been tagged along to the name of my father-in-law to justify the action.

When Aanisa and I were ordered to come out of the bedroom, it was 7.00 p.m. We sat in the lobby and a member of the raiding party switched on our television. Various news channels were reporting the raid on my house. The Aaj Tak correspondent, Deepak Chaurasia, stood outside our building, posing in front of my mail box with my name prominently displayed on it, and reported 'live' that I was absconding. Obviously he was not aware that I was still in the house. He reported that the police had discovered a laptop with incriminating evidence. Chaurasia had been well and truly misled by these overzealous IB officials, I thought. Later on he saw through this sinister game plan and actively participated in the campaign launched by the journalist fraternity to oppose my detention.

The news reports baffled me. Where had the laptop I was supposed to own come from? I asked Sahai about the 'document' they had recovered from my residence and about the laptop. He said that he did not know what these reporters were talking about. He assured me no such document had been recovered.

'You are a journalist yourself—surely you know how news is manufactured,' he said sarcastically.

The atmosphere had changed. The Income Tax officials were relaxed now. The lady officer, a tall, pretty young woman from the Indian Revenue Service, who had forced her entry into our bedroom in the early hours, was now chatting with Aanisa. She was quite different from the woman who had interrogated my wife at her father's residence. Women have their own way of interacting with each other. Once the barriers are broken, they have a lot to talk about. Aanisa asked her about her job, how she got into it and a lot more.

'Did you have a problem finding our house?' I heard Aanisa ask the woman officer. Had I not been at the receiving end of the law, I would have had a good laugh. I merely stared at her with an impassive face.

In the lobby, the Income Tax officials were finalizing their paperwork. They asked Aanisa and me to sign some papers. We did so obediently. Later on I came to know that they had made us sign the papers stating that they were signed under oath, when in fact neither had they administered any oath nor had these statements been recorded in the manner in which they said they were done.

A heated debate about me was going on in my study. By this time I was totally confused. And exhausted.

An officer came to me and asked if I would be able to give them a published copy of the file 'Forces' recovered from my computer. 'Please provide a copy of the published version of this file in a day or two. These people are planning to arrest you,' he said, sounding sympathetic.

I assured him that the document was indeed published and that I would submit a published copy to him. One of his colleagues came to me after the IB official had left and said, 'Why are you wasting your energy trying to convince them? They have come for you—they shall get you.'

The mere mention of the word 'giraftari' (arrest) caused Aanisa to panic. She rushed up to Sahai and asked, 'Are you arresting him?'

'No, we are not arresting him—we do not have power to,' Sahai assured her.

Aanisa was not convinced. She turned to Majid, who looked like the commander of the whole operation.

'Do not worry. Nothing is going to happen,' he said.

Around 9.00 p.m. Rajbir Singh, Assistant Commissioner, Delhi Police (Special Cell) emerged from my study. Since I had not seen him earlier, I gathered that he must have come to my flat when Aanisa and I had been locked in the bedroom. He signalled to a plainclothes man and, pointing towards me, said, 'Tell him to pack his belongings.'

I realized that they had indeed come for me.

Three
Smoke and Mirrors

The search operation was officially over. The Intelligence Bureau sleuths had persuaded the Delhi Police to do their bidding and, satisfied that the operation was a success, departed. Soon after, Rajbir Singh left, followed by his team.

However the officers of the Income Tax Department had to complete certain formalities. When they left after taking Aanisa's and my signatures on some papers, it was past 10.00 p.m. I looked around my house. It was in a shambles. Books, papers, newspaper clippings, clothes and household articles were strewn around. It seemed as if a rampaging mob had stormed through it. Was this the kind of training the department gives its investigating officers, I wondered.

I did not realize that two plainclothes officers had remained behind. They were Inspector Raman Lamba and Assistant Sub-Inspector (ASI) N.S. Rana. 'Is there anything more you need?' I asked them. Aanisa was terrified. 'Are you going to arrest him?'

'No, no, it's nothing serious. We just want him to accompany us to the police station for some questioning,' Inspector Lamba assured her. Just then my phone rang. They allowed me to receive the call. It was Asha Khosa of the *Indian Express*. The news of the recovery of a 'defence document' at my place had spread, she said, and wanted to know what was going on. I explained everything to her briefly and emphasized that the document did not contain classified information. That was the last phone call I was to receive for a long time.

Soon after Inspector Lamba asked me to change and go with them. ASI Rana gave Aanisa the telephone numbers of the Special Cell, Delhi Police at Lodhi Colony, in case she needed to contact me and once again told her that they would send me back as soon as they finished asking me some questions.

I had seen how the television channels had sensationalized the report of the raid at my place. It looked to me as if they had been fed all the information by the IB officials. Even now they would be waiting outside, looking for 'breaking news' and 'exclusive reports' at my expense. That they were reducing me to a tamasha, damaging my reputation and my dignity in the process, was of no consequence to them. Therefore I requested Inspector Lamba to arrange a quiet departure. He agreed and asked me which alternative route we could take. There was none. The only route leading out of the compound was swarming with cameras, microphones and mediapersons, hungry for photographs, images, sound bytes, anything to lend credibility to their stories. Finally it was decided that we would leave the premises in as casual a manner as possible, as if we were some government officials leaving the building. The policemen would not lock fingers with me, as they normally do when they escort someone to a police station. The ploy worked. No one got a whiff of our identity and we quietly slipped into a Maruti car and drove away.

Aanisa was all alone. Sitting amid the scattered household items, she did not know what to do. The state of her mind seemed to reflect the condition of our house. Emotionally drained and utterly confused, she went to the balcony and called a neighbour. The lady came out but immediately her husband summoned her inside. And that's how it was to remain for the next several months. Until the media highlighted my innocence, Aanisa and my children had to live like outcastes in the locality. Doors were shut in their faces and children pulled away and locked up inside their homes if they dared to venture into the compound.

Just as Aanisa was about to give in to her despair, a plainclothes man came to the door and told her that he was from the Delhi Police and was there to look after her. Very politely he said that he would be outside the house and she could seek his help in case of any difficulty. Obviously, the Delhi Police had decided to keep me, though they had told Aanisa that I would be sent back in a few hours.

By the time we reached the Special Cell of the Delhi Police at Lodhi Colony it was 10.30 p.m. I was taken to a room adjacent to Inspector Lamba's. Majid was there. With a malicious grin on his face, he sneered, 'Ab raho choudah saal andar.' (Now you can stay inside for 14 years.)

One of the officers present in the room found his remark in bad taste and retorted, 'Oh, so now you have become the Chief Justice of India? You will pronounce the judgement too?' I felt grateful to him for his intervention.

My hands and feet were cold. I was confident I had done nothing wrong, but then, in the presence of such overbearing authority, even the strongest person can crumble. Besides I had heard about the Special Cell of the Delhi Police. It was created to deal with terrorist-related cases and every time there was news of an arrest or an encounter with a terrorist, the media spotlighted its officers and their efficacy. As a result, the cell had earned a dreaded reputation. How many of these arrests and encounters were genuine is a matter of conjecture.

One of the familiar faces on television and in the newspapers was ACP Rajbir Singh, dubbed 'encounter specialist' by the media. That's how I recognized him when I saw him at my house. His tall, fair, sturdy appearance and his authoritarian manner would send a chill down the spine of anyone in his custody. But Rajbir Singh turned out to be completely contrary to stereotype. He was a gentleman officer who insisted on going by the rule book.

The room next to Inspector Lamba's office looked innocuously simple, with just a few chairs and a table. It was actually an interrogation room, fully soundproofed, equipped with a heavy-duty air conditioner, two mysterious black screens on the wall and powerful electric bulbs. I learned later that the temperature in the room could be varied from a freezing sub-zero to a scorching 60 degrees Celsius. Fortunately I was spared the experience of its capabilities.

I was escorted to the room and asked to sit on one of the chairs. I heard ACP Rajbir Singh tell Inspector Lamba, ASI Rana and Sub-Inspector (SI) Ashok Kumar that I was not to be subjected to any ill treatment as I had been arrested for political reasons. And then he went away, escorted by the other three.

A young constable came into the room and asked rather crudely, 'Tera naam kya hai?' I told him my name. He asked me to show him whatever I had and proceeded to list all the items on a piece of paper. This is what is called jama talashi, personal search.

A few moments later Inspector Lamba, SI Ashok Kumar and ASI Rana came back to the room. Inspector Lamba wanted to know who was going to be on night duty. He was told that it was SI Ashok Kumar and another policeman. Turning to Ashok Kumar, Inspector Lamba said, 'See that there is no harassment. He will remain here tonight—just arrange for a blanket.'

Soon I was left alone in the room and I stretched out on the floor. But sleep was the last thing on my mind. In utter confusion and despair, I tried to figure out what would happen next. But my mind refused to think clearly. Sometime during the night I must have dozed off, for it was 5.00 a.m. when SI Ashok Kumar came and woke me up. He asked me to freshen up and offered me some tea. It was a full twenty-four hours since the last cup of tea I had had.

SI Ashok Kumar had prepared the report during the night. Apparently the investigation process had begun. These officers were doing the groundwork to seek my remand from the court. Perhaps they felt that presenting the 'defence document' was not sufficient enough for the purpose.

The document recovered from my computer was not a secret one. It was actually three annexures of an article downloaded from the Internet years ago. The original document had been published by the Institute of Strategic Studies, Islamabad in the form of a booklet and was also available on their website. The institute is the Pakistani version of our Institute for Defence Studies and Analyses (IDSA). It had started a series of publications called 'Islamabad Paper Series'. In January 1996, it published a paper entitled 'Denial of Freedom and Human Rights: A Review of Indian Repression in Kashmir' by Dr Nazir Kamal.

Dr Kamal's paper mainly discussed the human rights situation in Kashmir, quoting various Indian and international human rights organizations like the Committee for Initiative on Kashmir (New Delhi), the Peoples Union for Civil Liberties (New Delhi), the Human Rights Commission (Srinagar), the International Human Rights Organization (Ludhiana, India) and the Institute of Kashmir Studies (Srinagar).

Commenting on the presence of security forces there, the paper alleges that there are 600,000 Indian security personnel in the state. 'In Srinagar itself, approximately 77,000 security forces are deployed, while in the Valley as a whole there are over 100,000 army soldiers and about 138,000 paramilitaries, making an overall total of more than 240,000 security forces. Thus, in the Valley, there are more than a hundred security personnel for every one square mile of territory. The deployment in Jammu exceeds 225,000 security personnel, consisting of more than 160,000 paramilitary forces and over 62,000 regular army soldiers.'

Dr Kamal termed Kashmir as 'the most militarised area in the world'. To support his contention, he annexed several appendices with the paper. The seven annexures dealt with the strength and deployment of army and paramilitary forces at various places in Jammu and Kashmir. Dr Kamal stated that these annexures had been provided by Pakistani Foreign Minister, Sardar Assef Ahmad, at a press conference on 14 July 1995. Dr Kamal also refers to the figures given by M.K. Narayan, former intelligence chief of India, and the Voice of America.

Since the theme of the research paper was the human rights situation in Jammu and Kashmir, it discussed causalities, arrests and displacements, torture and custodial killings, rapes, disappearances, draconian laws etc.

Forty-eight pages long in the printed version, the paper had ten chapters and seven annexures. The titles of the chapters were 'An Overview', 'Indian Military Presence in IHK', 'Casualties in IHK', 'Arrested and Displaced', 'Torture and Custodial Killings', 'Curfew and Crackdowns', 'Rape as an Instrument of Repression', 'Legalisation of Human Rights Abuses', 'Administrative Breakdown' and 'Summary'.

The seven annexures were entitled 'Annex-A: Fact Sheet on Indian Forces in Indian-held Kashmir', 'Annex-B: Latest Data on Indian Troops in Indian-held Kashmir', 'Annex-C: Indian Para-military Forces in IHK (District Wise)', 'Annex-D: Additional Inductions in IHK (last two months)', 'Annex-E: List of Torture Cells in Indian-held Kashmir in 1992D', 'Annex-F: Additional Army Interrogation Camps in Srinagar in 1992 (in Srinagar City Alone)' and 'Annex-G: UN Declaration on the Protection of All Persons from Enforced Disappearance'.

Since the document had been downloaded from the website of the Institute of Strategic Studies, Pakistan, it had used the term 'Indian-held Kashmir' wherever there was any reference to the state of Jammu and Kashmir.

The document attached to my charge sheet was a doctored version of this paper. Apparently, the sleuths of the IB had started tampering with the document while they were in my house, when I was locked inside the bedroom with Aanisa. On top of the document, which was in a WordStar format, they inserted the line 'ONLY FOR REFERENCE, STRICTLY NOT FOR PUBLICATION OR CIRCULATION'. Furthermore, they changed the term 'Indian-Held Kashmir' to 'Jammu and Kashmir'. The document presented to the Delhi Police consisted only of Annexures A, B and C as a self-contained database. They removed the annexure numbers, without which it looked like a classified document. On the basis of this tampered document, I was charged with a criminal case under the Official Secrets Act, 1923.

I was accused of acting as an agent of the ISI, the Inter Services Intelligence of Pakistan, collecting and passing on information on the deployment of Indian Army and other security forces in Jammu and Kashmir.

Throughout the court proceedings, the document was kept in a sealed cover and my lawyers and I were not allowed to see it. I had repeatedly told the IB men, as well as the Delhi Police, that it was part of a published document and I had stored it in my computer only for reference purposes, but to no avail.

The IB officers came up with another document against me to persuade the court that I was an insider of the Hizb-ul-Mujahideen as well. This document was actually a note circulated by Indian intelligence officers among the journalists reporting on Kashmir. News reports based on this inspired note had appeared in several newspapers. The note was eventually dropped when the charge sheet was filed.

At the time, I was utterly perplexed at being targeted with such vindictiveness. As a journalist working for the *Kashmir Times* and the *Daily Times* of Pakistan, I was reporting on sensitive issues related to Kashmir. I had been reporting on incidents and events without any fear or favour, unmindful of the interests of the parties involved. Some IB officials had found a few of my reports in the *Kashmir Times* unpalatable. It was only later that I realized I was paying for doing my job.

My marriage to the daughter of Syed Ali Shah Geelani, a top Hurriyat leader, came in handy for them. They clubbed me with him and tried to kill two birds with one stone. This strengthened their case and they were able to persuade the government to go along with their game.

Piecing together information I gathered from various sources, I was able to reconstruct the events of that fateful day when my house was raided. The IB informed the Delhi Police at around 3.00 p.m. that a case of espionage had been discovered. ACP Rajbir Singh, Inspector Ram Mehar Singh and other officials of the Delhi Police arrived at my residence. Inspector Ram Mehar Singh expressed his reluctance to handle the case since he had not previously dealt with a case under the Official Secrets Act, 1923 (OS Act).

So the search for another officer of the Delhi Police started. Inspector Madanjit Singh of the Special Branch, who was handling cases under the OS Act, was summoned to my residence. Inspector Madanjit Singh saw the file 'Forces' and opined that he saw no instance of violation of the OS Act. He refused to register the case and arrest me and suggested that the document be seized and sent to the Directorate General of Military Intelligence (DGMI) for an opinion. Only if the DGMI maintained that the document was a secret one and could have adverse implications for the security of the country could a criminal case against me be registered, he said. He was asked to leave.

Majid, who was present during the raid through the day, made a phone call to Joshi, a deputy director with the IB, who was in charge of the entire operation, taking place simultaneously at Srinagar and Delhi. Bypassing his immediate superiors, he had informed S.M. Gauba, a DCIO (Counter Espionage) in another section of the IB, equal in rank to an assistant commissioner of police, of his prize catch.

Gauba landed at my house during the raid and took a copy of the document. Before long, word of this operation had gone out to Kamal Pandey, then Home Secretary, and L.K. Advani, the home minister, as well.

Majid and Gauba still hadn't found an officer of the Delhi Police to assist them. They asked ACP Rajbir Singh to find someone suitable. Finally Inspector Raman Lamba was chosen to handle the case. He reached my house at around 8.00 p.m. I was sitting in the lobby at that time.

From there I could hear clearly some of the discussions going on in my study. The abusive language being used by some IB officials made me very uncomfortable as my wife was also there with me. The main topic of discussion was the nature of the seized document. I overheard ACP Rajbir Singh asking how the document could be classified as secret—I was a journalist and could have written it myself. Inspector Lamba scrutinized the document and said that he wanted to ask me some questions.

Then Gauba said they would have to arrest me as word had already gone to the home minister and the media had reported the recovery of an important defence document.

He called his superiors and informed them that the Delhi Police was refusing to arrest me without an opinion from the DGMI. Gauba's superiors, without caring to see the document, persuaded the Home Secretary to call Ajai Raj Sharma, Commissioner, Delhi Police to intervene. ACP Rajbir Singh was left with no option but to ask Inspector Lamba to register a criminal case and arrest me.

That is how I ended up in the Special Cell of the Delhi Police. The investigation had begun. I was finger-printed, foot-printed and photographed from every possible angle. The IB officials had invaded the police station and Inspector Lamba was being lectured about the manner in which he must move against me. Inspector Lamba told Gauba that I had insisted the document was a published one and that I would try to produce a printed copy of the document for him.

'He will never be able to produce it,' Gauba said confidently. 'Just proceed as directed and do not harbour any doubts in your mind.'

Around 8.00 a.m. Aanisa arrived at the police station. Gauba gave her a copy of the arrest memo and asked her to sign it.

'Are you really arresting him?' she asked almost disbelievingly.

Feigning total helplessness and humility Gauba replied, 'What can we do, the law is blind.'

As she signed the arrest memo, Aanisa retorted, 'Yes, I have also heard that the law is blind but I did not realize how blind. Actually it is you people who are blind.'

Aanisa had been allowed to bring me some food, and that was some comfort. She told me that the media were present in full strength outside the police station. I requested Inspector Lamba not to parade me before them. But some policemen, eager to see their faces on television and in the newspapers, took me out and posed in the full glare of flashbulbs.

I was produced before Sangita Dhingra Sehgal, the Chief Metropolitan Magistrate (CMM), Delhi. She asked me about the document recovered from me. I told her that these people were needlessly excited over a published document. It was not a secret one, I added. But my statement was not recorded. The court remanded me to police custody for five days.

This five-day police remand had been sought at the behest of some IB officials, I found out later. Their intention was to take me to Jammu, plant some RDX on me and then show that they had recovered RDX from me. Arrangements for the RDX as well as independent witnesses had already been made. In the meantime, the IB had managed to obtain a doctored opinion on the document from the DGMI. A deputy commissioner of police saw this communication from the DGMI and informed the IB officials that they could abandon their plans to take me to Jammu. The opinion from the DGMI was enough to keep me behind bars for a full five years. The IB officials readily agreed to drop their plans. I must mention here that it was also the efforts of some of my journalist friends who had sought an assurance from

L.K. Advani that I would not be taken to Kashmir nor would I be subjected to any third-degree treatment that spared me. Though Advani was not convinced of my innocence, he instructed the concerned officials according to the requests of my friends.

The rest of the day was uneventful. I was kept in a room in the rear of the Special Cell building.

The next day, 11 June, Aanisa and my friend Aunohita Mojumdar came to see me. Both looked worried. Aunohita came straight to the point. 'What did you say in court?' she asked. I told her about my conversation with the CMM. Just then a policeman rushed into the room and asked her to leave.

But then a prominent daily had carried a report saying that I had admitted before the court that I was working for the ISI. I was even quoted as saying that Syed Ali Shah Geelani had married his daughter to me because he was happy with my jehadi work.

The IB had widely publicized me as a big catch. Many newspapers had carried a photograph of the policemen posing with me, their prize. The photograph was to provide me with some entertainment. One of the policemen told me that a colleague of his received a phone call from his home in western Uttar Pradesh, informing him that his picture had appeared in the local edition of *Dainik Jagran*. His five-year-old nephew came on the line. 'Uncle, you caught that terrorist? I don't believe it. You cannot even catch a chicken here, let alone me!'

There was no interrogation for the whole day, though some time later Majid did come to the police station. Inspector Lamba asked him, in my presence, why no IB official was coming to interrogate me. Majid said his job was done. Others would take care of my case. He had bigger fish to fry.

That night, after dinner, I was escorted to the Lodhi Colony Police Station and deposited in the lock-up. There was no fan or

electric bulb inside the room. It took my eyes a few moments
to get used to the dark. When I looked around the cell I noticed
a frail young man whimpering in pain. He was Altaf Wani, a
small-time Kashmiri shawl vendor. The police had found a million
dollar note on him. The police perhaps did not know the United
States government had never issued such a note and that it had
value only as a souvenir. In his statement to the court, Wani
said the police had planted fake currency notes amounting to
25,000 rupees and two kilograms of RDX on him. Wani told
me that he had been picked up twelve days ago while he was on
his way to the airport. In the records, he was reportedly arrested
from Lahori Gate.

Altaf Wani told me he had been severely tortured during
the day. He was kept naked in sub-zero temperature, had ice
cold water poured on him and was then mercilessly beaten. The
policemen did not ask him any questions and he was genuinely
perplexed about why he was being tortured like this. Altaf Wani
remained in jail till I was released.

On 12 June Aanisa managed to trace a photocopy of the
published version of Dr Nazir Kamal's paper. She wanted to
submit the document to the police, but was afraid that the
document would not be placed on record. She was assured that
Dr K.K. Paul, joint commissioner and in-charge of the Special
Cell, was an upright officer and would not allow any harm to
come to the document. Only then did Aanisa submit the
document to the police. Once again it was sent to the DGMI
for its opinion. The DGMI took six months to get back with
their views on it. But that's another matter.

The presence of the published version of the allegedly
incriminating document caused consternation among the IB
officials pursuing the case. They had searched my house

thoroughly and found no trace of it. And now here it was. The Special Cell was literally under siege. A number of IB sleuths descended on its premises. The police officials were trying to persuade them to drop the case since no offence was made out. From my room, which was adjacent to Inspector Lamba's, I heard ACP Rajbir Singh tell them the published version had made things crystal clear. But Gauba, Majid and company were in no mood to relent. While they agreed that no offence was made out, I could not be released so easily.

ACP Rajbir Singh stood his ground. He tried explaining to them that since I was a journalist, many journalists were taking a keen interest in this case. He made it clear that he would pursue the case only on the basis of available evidence. He said they would send the documents to the DGMI for their opinion. Gauba wasn't pleased.

That afternoon an IB official came to meet me. He was an elderly gentleman, pleasant and polite. He asked me nothing pertaining to the document. Rather, he seemed more keen to explain to me his methods of interrogation. One of his favourites was to insert chilli powder into the rectum of an accused. In vivid detail he explained what a person feels when subjected to third-degree methods, and claimed that they had been perfected in India. Of the vast variety of torture techniques, he said, most are simple and brutal. Others are far more sophisticated and use technology to maximize pain and leave few signs.

This was my introduction to third-degree methods commonly used while interrogating suspects. While I was in police custody several IB officials elaborated on these methods, which I would have dismissed as bragging had it not been for the accounts of my fellow inmates in Tihar Jail later on. Even those who had been picked up on mere suspicion were inhumanly tortured.

What was shocking was that these torture techniques are not used as a last resort to break a stubborn criminal's silence. They are applied in the first instance itself. To give you an idea of some of these horrors, I will briefly describe a few. One method is to tie the individual's hands behind his back, then place a pipe or rod behind his knees and lift him up with the help of the rod, just above ground level so that the knees support the entire body weight.

Hanging a person upside down and then beating him on the soles of the feet is another common practice. Rolling a smooth round post like a rolling pin over a prone body may sound harmless but can be very painful, according to one who experienced it.

Using blinding lights to keep a suspect awake is an old yet popular method. A former official of Uttar Pradesh's Local Intelligence Unit told me in jail that he was not allowed to sleep for seven days continuously by his interrogators at the torture cell in Delhi's Red Fort. In this same category is the practice of subjecting the bare-bodied individual to extreme temperatures. Again no telltale signs are visible; it is very effective and so a convenient and preferred method.

But torture need not be only physical. For many, their threshold of pain may be very high but the humiliation of being paraded naked before members of one's family and friends and the interrogators is far more difficult to endure.

Thank God I was not subjected to any of the above treatments. Merely hearing about these accounts had terrified me; I cannot even imagine what would have happened if I had been put through any of them. Perhaps that's what my interrogator, the polite gentleman, was trying to do: frighten me into submission.

Anyway, he changed the topic and proceeded to ask me about my visit to Pakistan. Everything about that trip had been well documented in my travelogue for the *Kashmir Times*, and the news portal *Tehelka*, but I recounted it for him nevertheless. This gentleman had been part of the advance team that went to Pakistan before Prime Minister Atal Bihari Vajpayee's visit to Lahore.

The following day, 13 June 2002, two more interrogators joined him. They were from the Kashmir Cell of the IB. One of them was a tall, hefty fellow who tried unsuccessfully to speak to me in English. He was the only one at the Special Cell who kept threatening and abusing me. He tried to extract information regarding my contacts at the Pakistan High Commission. The other officer delighted in narrating stories about his interrogations of militants in Punjab and took pains to explain to me the difference between militancy in Punjab and militancy in Kashmir.

On 14 June my editor Prabodh Jamwal and an advocate, V.K. Ohri, visited me. The *Kashmir Times* had taken up my case. They were convinced that I was innocent and had been framed by some interested sections in the government. Hence they were confident that I would be free soon, probably the next day itself, when the five-day period in police custody would end. Little did they know about the behind-the-scenes manoeuvring that was going on.

It will be in order to recapitulate the sequence of events of the past few days and their repercussions.

On 9 June the IB sleuths had handed over a printout of the tampered document recovered from my computer to the Delhi Police. On 10 June the police had sent the printout to the DGMI for an opinion on the nature of the said document. On 12 June a photocopy of the published version of the document had been handed over to the IB. Since the police had received no response from DGMI till then, they delivered the published version to the DGMI the same day.

On 14 June, Inspector Raman Lamba received a letter from Lt Col Ramesh Sharma of GSO 1, MI-9. It acknowledged receipt of the copy of the published version as well as the printout of the document. However the opinion enclosed made no reference to the published version and referred only to the 9 June document, which was the doctored version of the file retrieved from my computer. The letter stated, 'The opinion of DGMO/ MO3 on documents (Fact Sheet on Army and Para Military Forces in J&K) recovered from Syed Iftikhar Gilani on 09 Jun 2002 is enclosed in original for your perusal and action as deemed fit please.'

Whenever the DGMI is called upon to give an opinion on any seized documents relating to the armed forces, it takes a few weeks, sometimes even months, before it renders its opinion on the matter. Obviously there is a set procedure to be followed.

In my case, though the DGMI had been requested to give its opinion on the document, it was the Directorate General of Military Operations (DGMO) which responded.

It seemed as if my interrogators had finished their questioning. They would now come just to chat and register their presence. A group of people came and asked me about Jammu and Kashmir, its economy, annual plan, geography etc. I was astonished by their questions, wondering what they had to do with my case. I was told that they were not part of my interrogation team but wanted this information since they were preparing for a departmental examination for promotion and Jammu and Kashmir was an important subject for intelligence agencies. They had approached me since they knew that I was a good source on Kashmir in Delhi.

Meanwhile ACP L.N. Rao had taken over the case from ACP Rabjir Singh. One evening I was taken to his room. He asked me if I had any bank accounts with Standard Chartered Bank and Development Credit Bank. I said I had none. Then he accused me of being a smuggler, and said that the Income Tax Department had found 750 grams of gold jewellery in my locker. I said I did not know of any such jewellery and gave him the details of the bank accounts I held. I was sent back to my room.

After a brief respite, I was summoned once again to the interrogation room. The IB officer had some papers in his hand. He asked me about some Imtiyaz Bazaz and G.M. Bhat, a former Hurriyat Conference office bearer. These documents later resurfaced in the court, but were withdrawn when we insisted that they be probed and the truth be unearthed.

On 15 June I was produced before J.P.S. Malik, Additional Chief Metropolitan Magistrate, Delhi. My lawyer Ohri filed an application for my discharge and release on the grounds that the document was from a public source and was available on the Internet. He provided a photocopy of the published version of the document. The photocopy clearly showed that the ministry of foreign affairs, Pakistan was the source of information. The judge rejected the request of the prosecution to conduct the proceedings in camera. But the prosecution made the plea that the document that had been submitted by us was only a photocopy of the published version and hence could not be relied on, whereupon J.P.S. Malik remanded me to judicial custody and asked my counsel to produce the original copy of the publication. He asked the prosecution to file their reply by 18 June 2002. The case was adjourned to 2 July 2002.

It was ordered that I be transferred to the dreaded Tihar Central Jail.

Four
Life In Tihar

It was at the Tis Hazari Courts on a hot, sultry summer day, 18 June 2002, that I was handed over to the 3rd Battalion of the Delhi Armed Police. They are entrusted with the job of escorting prisoners from jail to court and back. One of the Special Cell officers handed me a food packet before I was herded into the bus that transported prisoners to Tihar Jail. The bus is actually a cage on wheels. It has wooden benches on either side with an open space in the centre. Some prisoners sit on the benches while others stand in the centre with nothing to hold on to as the bus jolts along the bumpy Delhi roads. At both ends are narrow openings with grills. Once all the prisoners enter through the rear door the grill-shutter is drawn and firmly locked. A few armed constables sit outside the grill.

Holding the food packet in my hand, I stumbled into the cage. Before I could regain my breath, several prisoners pounced on me. It took me a few seconds to realize that they were after my food packet. I quickly threw it away to save myself from their assault. The packet burst and dal makhani and subzi were strewn all over the floor. My fellow passengers almost licked every morsel of the food off the floor. 'It's been a year since we got the taste of properly seasoned food,' said one of the prisoners, licking his lips. It was pathetic and ludicrous at the same time. I was reminded of some shrines where monkeys snatch sweetmeats and offerings from the hands of devotees. But this was neither a pilgrimage nor was the place I was heading to a shrine. Already I had been given a feel of Tihar Ashram, as the former prison chief Kiran Bedi preferred to call it, and the sages and their disciples who inhabited it.

After almost a hundred prisoners were packed into the cage, the driver started the bus. I must have appeared genteel and out of place, for one of them made space for me to sit down. Sandwiched between them on the hard wooden seat, I felt that my experience of travelling in crowded DTC buses had come in handy. Slowly I looked around. Many of the passengers looked familiar. They had evil expressions and angry scars on their faces. I had seen them, or rather villains like them, in innumerable Hindi films. A few, though, looked innocent. I could tell who the old-timers were from the way they were terrorizing the first-timers, and my heart began to thud. The man sitting beside me asked me my name. 'Oh, Gilani. Hmm…you will be lodged at Jail No. 3,' he said to me. My first lesson in the functioning of the prison system: inmates are dumped in different jails based on their surnames.

The Tihar Central Jail complex consists of seven jails. It was transferred from the Delhi Gate area in North Delhi to its current location, in Tihar village in West Delhi, in 1958. Initially only one Central Jail with a lodging capacity for 1267 prisoners was commissioned. As the prison population grew it was bifurcated and Central Jail No. 2 and Central Jail No. 3 were carved out of it in 1984 and 1985 respectively. Jail No. 2 is now meant for convicts sentenced to rigorous imprisonment. It has factories, where bread, biscuits and other products are made. A new Camp Jail No. 4 was started in 1978 and was converted into the full-fledged Central Jail No. 4 with a lodging capacity of 740 prisoners in 1990. In March 1996 Central Jail No.5 was built specifically for 750 male prisoners between the ages of sixteen and twenty-one. On 3 June 2000 another jail exclusively for women, with a capacity of 400, was opened. The total lodging capacity of the six Central Prisons in Tihar Jail Complex is 3637, whereas the number of prisoners lodged was 12,232 as on 31 March 2003. Separate wards for mothers-in-law and sisters-in-law booked for demanding dowry, women arrested under the Immoral Traffic law, drug pedlars—usually foreigners—and others have also been created. Owing to the extent of the jurisdiction of the jail, the post of Inspector General (Prisons) was upgraded to that of Director General (Prisons) in December 2001.

It took us almost an hour to reach the imposing gates of the Tihar Jail complex. Our first stop was Jail No.1. After unloading the prisoners meant for this jail, a policeman called my name and told me to get ready to alight at the next stop. At Jail No. 3, I, along with ten to twelve other prisoners, got out of the cramped bus. Policemen stood on either side of a narrow wicket gate and we were made to go through it. I was the last one to enter. The others were sitting down in rows in the space between two huge gates, one leading to the outside world and the other opening into the main jail with its labyrinth of wards and barracks. This space, which houses the administrative block of the jail, is called the 'deodhi'. All activity here is monitored on closed-circuit television. On a blackboard hanging on the wall were some statistics showing the number of prisoners lodged in the jail. There were also some tables that were rather high, which meant that the officers had to work at them standing up. A corridor on one side of this hall leads to the offices of the superintendent, the deputy superintendents and the record room. On the other side is the corridor leading to the mulaqat room, or reception, for family members who come to visit.

As soon as I entered I heard murmurs from around the desk of the jail official checking the names of the incoming prisoners.

'He has come,' one official said to another. The man went inside. He soon returned and asked me to follow him. He led me to a room adjacent to the jail superintendent's office, called the 'undertrial office'.

One Assistant Superintendent Kishan was sitting on a chair behind a table. Ten to twelve others were in the room. Some seemed to be jail staff, while others appeared to be inmates. Assistant Superintendent Kishan asked my name. Before I had finished saying it, a Nepali staffer slapped me. It was the signal for a free-for-all. I was kicked from behind, blows rained on my back and someone grabbed my hair and banged my head against the table. Blood started oozing from my mouth. My nose and ears started bleeding too. Accompanying these blows were the choicest abuses.

'Sala, gaddar, Pakistani agent,' they were screaming. 'People like you should not be allowed to live. Traitors should be hanged straightaway.'

For about half an hour I suffered this ghastly display of patriotism as both the officials and the jail inmates exhorted each other to show me the punishment for treason. Finally I lost consciousness. When I came to, I found myself dumped in the corridor outside, with fresh blood stains on my face. I was told to go and wash my face. A barrage of abuses followed me to the bathroom. Suddenly a voice thundered, 'Clean the toilet.'

It was Rajesh (name changed), one of my tormentors, displaying his authority.

The toilet was as filthy as a public lavatory at a bus station. Before I could say anything, Rajesh ordered me to take off my blood-soaked shirt and clean the toilet with it. I had no choice but to obey him. It took me almost an hour to clean the toilet.

Barely had I finished when Ramu (name changed), another convict, loomed over me like an executioner, and ordered me to bring an enormous cooler lying some distance away and fix it near the room. Despite all my efforts, the cooler did not budge. A Tamil Nadu Special Police (TNSP) personnel was moved by my plight and asked some of the new prisoners to help me.

Only later did I learn that Rajesh and Ramu, who sought to give me lessons in patriotism right through my stay in Tihar Jail, had been convicted for far more heinous crimes. Rajesh was facing charges of triple murder and was later sentenced to a total of eighty years of rigorous imprisonment. Ramu, an undertrial, was accused of rape and later sentenced.

The corridor was now jam-packed with new prisoners sitting on the floor, waiting for admission formalities to commence. The adjacent room was unlocked. Again I was summoned and ordered to clean the room and the tables and chairs inside. I obeyed unquestioningly.

Admission proceedings began. One by one the new prisoners were called inside. A jail official and a doctor were doing the job with the help of a few favoured prisoners.

Obviously Rajesh and Ramu were among the favoured lot. Rajesh was with the doctor. As he recorded my name and identification marks, he let loose a volley of verbal and physical abuse. The doctor enquired about my offences. When he was told that I was an ISI agent, he too beat me up.

However, as a medical practitioner, he was there to give every new prisoner a thorough medical examination and record injuries, if any. He asked me to put down in writing that the injuries inflicted at the jail were actually caused by the police while I was in their custody. He expressed surprise that the police had let off a traitor like me so easily. For the first time I gathered some courage and refused to sign the report.

The doctor could not force me to do his bidding. I realized he could do nothing worse than hand me over to Rajesh, Ramu and company.

'Where is your shirt?' asked Ramu.

'In the bathroom,' I said.

'Go get it and wear it as it is,' he commanded.

The shirt was so filthy that I almost vomited. But I was forced to wear it for the next three days. That too in the sultry June heat of Delhi. Apparently such treatment is meted out to every prisoner who is perceived to have committed rape of minors or offences under the Official Secrets Act.

There was one final ritual of indignity and humiliation to go through before entering the jail: I was asked to strip along with other prisoners. Tihar Special Police (TSP) personnel rigorously check every part of the body for tobacco, drugs and other contraband that may be concealed on one's person. This examination is done every time a prisoner returns from the outside world, either from the mulaqat room or from court.

Generally every new entrant is sent to Mulahiza ward at least for one night, before he is assigned to the appropriate ward. This depends on whether the prisoner is first-timer or a repeater.

The high-security ward is called 'Highlight' in the jail. The inmate is locked up for twenty-three hours a day and not allowed to interact with anyone. He is only allowed to walk in the corridor for one hour in the day.

In the eyes of the jail administration I was a hard-core criminal. So I was marched straight to the high-security ward. A convict, clad in white shirt and trousers and holding some papers in his hands, told the ward in-charge to keep me in solitary confinement.

'Where shall I get a separate cell for him? I already have forty-five inmates here,' the in-charge complained. An argument between the in-charge and the convict followed. Leaving me with two TSP personnel keeping guard, the two of them went to the jail office. A few minutes later the in-charge was back.

Looking at me through narrowed eyes, he muttered, 'You are a very dangerous prisoner,' and led me through a maze of corridors, unlocking many doors till we came to the 'kaal kothari' or 'death cell'. This block was reserved for those awaiting execution.

I was thrust into a small cell measuring eight feet by six feet. It was completely bare except for a thick layer of dust. It had probably not hosted any inmate for years. Attached to it was a filthy toilet, which did not have doors or curtains. I was not even allowed the luxury of an hour's walk in the corridor. I was completely and utterly isolated. I did not see the face or hear the voice of any other prisoner. I had nothing to read, nothing to write on and no one to talk to. The true meaning of socialization and companionship dawned on me compellingly, and I realized that nothing was more dehumanizing than the absence of human company.

A few cells away was Prof. Davinderpal Singh Bhullar, awaiting execution of the death sentence awarded by a TADA court. Professor Bhullar had been deported to India from Germany on 18 January 1995. He was arrested at the Indira Gandhi airport and charged with falsification of government documents and two breaches of TADA. He was handed over to the Punjab Police in January 1995 for a period of two months. When Professor Bhullar was returned to judicial custody in March 1995 he lodged a complaint saying that he was physically tortured and threatened with execution if he did not sign several blank papers. He alleged that these blank signed papers were later used by the Punjab Police to falsify his confessional statement.

Professor Bhullar was sentenced to death by a Designated Court (special courts enacted under TADA) in August 2001. He then filed a petition with the Supreme Court of India. His appeal was heard in April 2002 by a three-judge bench which upheld the lower court ruling by a majority of two to one. The majority judgment found him guilty while the dissenting judgment acquitted him. According to the minority judgment, the police had failed to corroborate the confessional statement Professor Bhullar is said to have made before them.

By the time all the formalities were completed and I was installed in my cell it was late. Dinner had already been served to the inmates and I had to go without food. Sleep was miles away. I still believed that this was a bad dream and once I woke up, it would end and everything would be all right. I could find no reason to justify my detention in this block because, according to the Delhi Jail Manual, no prisoner except convicts awaiting the death sentence can be kept here.

Outside my cell was a brightly lit corridor. At one end was a guard. At the other end was a little gate which opened on to a small lawn, where executions took place. How many miserable souls must have walked this corridor on the way to the gallows. I believe not many went to the gallows on their own feet. They had to be dragged along. Others lost consciousness. I had noticed some guidelines on the execution of a death sentence written in a fading paint on the wall. It had sent a chill down my spine.

I was told later that on one side of this lawn was the grave of Mohammad Maqbool Bhat, a legendary leader of the Jammu and Kashmir Liberation Front (JKLF). He was hanged at that spot on 11 February 1984. Till February 2002 his grave was visible and some jail officials used to light candles and pray there. But now some construction work was being carried out at the site.

The next evening the warder unlocked my cell door and asked me to accompany him. He had to unlock and lock several doors before we came out. He led me straight to the office of the deputy superintendent, Veena Nukad, at the deodhi.

'Are you any relation of S.A.R. Geelani, an accused in the Parliament House terrorist attack?' she barked at me.

'No. Not at all,' I declared.

'But he says that you are his brother-in-law,' she retorted.

'I have never set eyes on him,' I stated vehemently.

Nukad told the warder to take me to the office of the jail superintendent, A.K. Kaushal. Kaushal was a tall, lean fellow. He instructed the warder to remain outside his room and then turned to me. 'How are you feeling now?' he asked.

I described to him the torture and humiliation that I had to endure at the time of my admission. I also explained my case in an attempt to impress upon him my innocence and convince him that I did not deserve the treatment meted out to me by the jail authorities. Shaking his head, he stated, 'But you have committed a very serious offence.' Again I presented him the details of the document recovered from me. Looking thoughtful, he told me to wait outside his room. Perhaps he was inclined to believe that I was not such a dangerous prisoner after all. He called for his personal assistant and issued some instructions to his subordinates. I was now led to the jail control room known as the 'chakkar'. All inmates dread the chakkar. It is used to keep the unruly elements in check.

The senior-most assistant superintendent, Thomas, an elderly South Indian gentleman, was sitting in the control room. He asked my name and other details and noted them down in a register. He was a very decent and polite person and his were the first kind words that I heard since my arrival in the jail.

I was given a ticket and told, 'Preserve this ticket. It is your ration card in the jail.' The ticket bore my name, FIR number and alleged offences. I was told I had been allotted a place in the Mulahiza ward, reserved for first-time prisoners, and escorted there. At the gate of the ward was another register and all the columns had to be duly filled once again.

The Mulahiza ward consists of ten barracks. The stated capacity of the ward was about 200, but when I was there it held around 500 inmates. No inmate is allowed to spend more than six months in this ward. If he is not out on bail within that time, he is sent to join the repeaters in other wards.

Of the ten barracks, Barracks Nos. 2 and 3 were meant for new entrants. Barracks No. 10 used to be a theatre during Kiran Bedi's tenure. But all that was left of it now was the dilapidated signboard that said 'Kiran Theatre'. It had become a barracks like any other, full beyond its capacity. All the new inmates were asked to line up in the middle. The barracks pradhan, or head, was one Davender, a young man accused of defrauding a bank. He and a couple of his associates were calling out our names one by one and writing them down. Soon my name was called. I was conscious that my shirt was filthy and smelly and could lead to trouble. I was right.

'You rascal, spreading filth everywhere. Can't you wear a clean shirt?' Davender and his associates shouted.

'Anyway, what's your name?' Davender asked me. I repeated my full name along with my father's name.

'Such a long name,' he said and slapped me across my face.

'It was not his fault! Blame his parents for it!' someone taunted and they all sniggered.

'Okay, under which section are you here?' he asked. I handed over my card. They could not make out what OS meant. A short, handsome young Kashmiri Pandit came forward but he too could not figure what OS was. Finally I decided to tell them. There was pandemonium. Apparently it was all part of the ragging tradition. More humiliation, more violence. When they had had their fun, they gave us a whole list of dos and don'ts. Then we, the new entrants, were told to find ourselves a place to sleep. When we entered the barracks I had caught sight of Altaf Wani, the Kashmiri shawl salesman who had been with me in the Special Cell. Altaf made some room for me. I was touched by his concern. Before I fell asleep I kept thinking of all the shlokas, lines from poetry and quotations adorning the drab brown walls of the prison. While they advocated compassion, a sense of service and respect for human life, one's dignity, self-respect and individuality were constantly violated even by those who were supposed to uphold them!

The following day, 20 June 2002, all the inmates were awakened at 5.30 a.m. by the warder, who yelled, *utho, utho* (arise, arise). This was how my day was to begin for the next seven months. One warder seemed to get sadistic pleasure in punishing the inmates. He would not call out to us, but would silently sneak into the cells. If he found someone still sleeping, he would make that person's life hell for the rest of that day. I became an early riser perforce.

Soon after our morning ablutions were completed, we were herded to the ground to say a prayer. It was a song from a famous V. Shantaram movie *Do Aankhen Barah Haath*. The film dealt with the issue of jail reforms. While the Tihar Jail authorities insisted on the prayer being sung every day, its message did not seem to have percolated into their thoughts and deeds. They used to keep a close watch on the prisoners and anyone found wanting in religious fervour was singled out for the most horrible punishment.

The lyrics of the song ask god to help us all, his servants, to tread the right path, do good deeds, and stay away from evil so that when we finally depart this earth our souls will be at peace. The singing of this prayer was introduced by Kiran Bedi, the zealous prison chief who tried very hard to bring about some reforms in the prison system and conditions of the prisoners. Today, the prayer is nothing but another form of punishment.

We were all given two loaves of bread made in the jail bakery and a badly prepared glass of tea. I had had no dinner and was desperately hungry, but I could not eat the bread or drink the tea—they were so bad. Utterly dejected, I was sitting on a small platform built around a tree in the yard when a tall, slim, middle-aged man came to me. He asked me if I was the same Iftikhar who was arrested under the Official Secrets Act. I replied in the affirmative. He introduced himself as Wasi Akhtar Zaidi, also charged with violation of the OS Act. Many other inmates surrounded me. They had all seen me on the television news channels and looked at me with sympathy. But a little later, inexplicably, news channels were blacked out from the television network.

Wasi Akhtar offered me tea from the jail canteen. He asked me if I was facing any problem. I requested him to get me shifted to some other barracks if possible, since I had been subjected to much harassment and humiliation there. The inmates used their clout with the ward munshi and got me transferred to Barracks No. 3. However the situation was no better there. Immediately upon arrival I was ordered to clean the toilet. After doing that I tried to take a nap. Suddenly an inmate, Nitin Panda (name changed), boxed my ear and made me get up. He took one look at my face and asked if I was the same Kashmiri who had been arrested from Malviya Nagar during an Income Tax raid. Oh no! What now, I wondered. Hesitantly I nodded. His reaction was nothing short of shocking. He became quite courteous and introduced me to the other inmates, and then took me to the pradhan. He told the pradhan and his associates and the other inmates to take good care of me and not harass me. The behaviour of the inmates changed dramatically. They showed me great respect and did not allow me to do any work in the barracks. I was astounded.

Much later I learned that an influential detainee, who had been released by the time I was taken in, had warned them not to harass me when I was brought to the prison. He had seen me on the television installed in the barracks. Knowing my name and the system of lodging at Tihar, these people knew beforehand that I would be brought to that ward.

As mentioned earlier, the prisoners are lodged according to their surnames. The classification system is quite interesting and bears illustration.

Jail No. 1	All prisoners whose surnames start with S and T, blood relatives and drug addicts.
Jail No. 2	All convicts.
Jail No. 3	All prisoners whose surnames start with A, B, C, D, E, G, H, I, L, V, W. Ailing prisoners from all wards and jails are admitted in the jail hospital here.

Jail No. 4	All prisoners whose surnames start with F, J, K, M, N, O, P, Q, R, U, X, Y and Z.
Jail No. 5	All prisoners in the age group eighteen to twenty years.
Jail No. 6	All female prisoners / convicts / undertrials.

Tihar Central Jail No. 3 has twelve wards. A ward is a section of the jail enclosed by high walls. It consists of a number of barracks which house the prisoners. Each barracks is like a dormitory and the number of inmates, usually between thirty and sixty, depends on the size and capacity of the barracks. Each barracks has walls on three sides with some small windows with strong grills perched high above. The fourth side is completely grilled with a tiny gate made of iron bars. This side offers a full view of the barracks to the patrolling jail officials. However because it is open the inmates are exposed to the vagaries of the weather. While there is only one common bathroom-cum-latrine for use during the lock-up period, the barracks have been provided with a few fans and a colour television set. The barracks also have a small shrine with some idols of Hindu gods and goddesses.

While Ward Nos. 1 and 2 are basically meant for convicts, a block in Ward No. 2 is reserved for punishing the kasoories, the unruly undertrials. They are usually in solitary confinement but it is common for kasoories to be put into the notorious and dreaded twenty cells of the jail hospital in Ward Nos. 3 and 4. These cells are completely isolated and house mentally deranged prisoners.

Ward Nos. 5 and 6 house repeaters and the others who have been in jail for more than six months. Ward No. 7 houses psychiatric patients and drug addicts. Ward No. 8 is the high-security ward. Ward No. 9 is reserved for those who wish to practice Vipaasana (meditation). Ward No. 10, the Mulahiza ward, houses first-timers for a period of six months. Ward No. 11 is called the IGNOU Ward. It has an authorized study centre of the Indira Gandhi National Open University (IGNOU) and National Open School (NOS). Ward No. 12 is the langar, the community kitchen for the whole jail except Ward No. 7 and the hospital, which have their own separate langars.

Kiran Bedi had abolished the class system in the jail. If on the surface the jail looks to be an egalitarian community, the administration has found ways to get around the system. It is flexible enough to provide comforts for those with money and muscle. Such people generally make their way to the IGNOU ward or Ward No. 7, which is a preferred place for the high and mighty as they get separate cells with drug addicts serving them. Besides it has its own langar where they get better food.

Racial discrimination is rampant in Tihar, I discovered. Foreigners, especially Europeans, were treated better than Indian inmates as they had money to spend. Most of the foreigners I saw were charged with narcotics trafficking under the Narcotics Drugs and Psychopathic Substances Act (NDPS Act). They got bread and milk, which were denied to the local inmates. They were not locked up during the day and were free to roam around in the jail complex. They were generally lodged at the IGNOU ward. Some of them even managed to get separate cells.

As I was neither a foreigner nor a rich and mighty individual, I was lodged with the ordinary inmates. The inmates at barracks No. 3 got so attached to me that they even stalled my transfer to another barracks when new entrants were admitted. They knew the system well.

But my troubles had not ended. I was free from harassment only inside the barracks. The moment the barracks were unlocked the harassment began in full swing. I was made to clean the general toilets, sweep and mop the floor and the common areas of the ward. The warders and the munshis seemed to have been instructed to inflict as much pain as they could.

The cliche that time passes slowly when one is idle and inactive was not true in my case. To me time seemed to have slowed down tremendously and the days appeared endless, despite being busy almost all the time in the Mulahiza ward. In the morning it was dusting and cleaning toilets, bathrooms and floors. After lunch, when everyone else was locked up and left alone to rest, I, along with a few other inmates, was sent to do manual labour at a construction site in the jail itself.

This routine continued for forty days. I had not worked so hard in my entire life. The work at the construction site was hell. Ever so often I reflected on the irony of the situation. Here I was, a journalist who used his fingers to wield a pen to disseminate information, educate and thereby emancipate the people, contributing to the nation-building process. But now the same fingers were engaged in building concrete structures meant to hold people in captivity. My hands had become rough and coarse and I had cuts and scratches everywhere. Surely my hands were not meant for this kind of constructive work?

But ironies were not my prerogative alone. I met a new entrant, a well-dressed man at the construction site. Ashwin Kumar (name changed) was an educated fellow, the son of an Air Force officer. Ashwin was one of many students arrested for participating in the anti-Mandal-Commission agitation around twelve years ago. He was a student at Delhi University at that time. Like other students, he too had protested against reservations for other backward classes. The students were kept in the lock-up for one day and then released. Ashwin went on to complete his education and moved to Jaipur, where he had found a job. In the meantime many cases related to the anti-Mandal-Commission agitation were withdrawn. Ashwin believed that the case against him too was withdrawn and, since no summons reached him, he did not bother to attend the court. One fine day a team from the Delhi Police descended on his home, picked him up and dumped him in Tihar Jail. He was declared a proclaimed offender. I was completely flummoxed by the way our hallowed system of law enforcement functioned. Ashwin told me that during his early days in jail he too was regularly beaten up. His offence: showing off his educational qualifications! Luckily for him, Ashwin was eventually released.

It was my third day in jail and no one had come to visit me. And it upset me. I had been wearing the same filthy clothes for three days, since I had nothing to change into. Finally I went to the social welfare officer, who is in charge of looking after the welfare of the inmates, counselling them and being in touch with their families. I told him that I was worried because no one, not even my wife, had come to meet me. The officer, Sanjay Kumar, told me that I should forget about the mulaqat. 'Your wife has also been arrested,' he said nonchalantly.

I was stunned. Once I got over the initial shock, a feeling of utter despair and helplessness overcame me. Aanisa's face swept into sharp focus before my eyes. I felt I could touch it if I put my hand out. There was a bleak and anxious expression on her face. I recalled the unfailing regularity with which she had visited me at the Special Cell and the court. But she had not been present in the court on the day I was sent to judicial custody. This gave credence to the statement of the social welfare officer.

Suddenly I was overwhelmed by the hopelessness of my situation. My predicament did not matter any longer. The thought of Aanisa being in jail devastated me.

I looked around. Amid the squalor and high decibel levels of the barracks I experienced the deathly silence of loneliness. It seemed like the end of the road. There was only misery and pain to look forward to. Suddenly, the smiling face of my wife appeared in front of me. She had come to my barracks, breaking all barriers. I did not know what to say to her. She did not say anything either. But just a glimpse of her smiling face had an inexpressible effect on me. It did not matter that she was not with me. It did not matter where I was sitting and what I was thinking. The turbulence disappeared. A deep calm entered my being. I was able to forget about my own wretched condition for a while.

Just then a convict munshi, Hari Singh, came to me and handed over coupons worth fifty rupees. 'Thomas saheb has sent it for you. He saw from the mulaqat register that you have not had any visit from your home, and so...' he trailed off. The act of kindness by Assistant Superintendent Thomas was most unexpected. I was deeply touched. People like him are a ray of sunshine in this dark world of ours, the small but sure thread of reassurance that despite the intensive rot in the system some people have managed to retain the inherent essence of humanity. This gift from Thomas was most timely and opportune. I did not have a single paisa at that time. For the first time I realized how precious fifty rupees could be.

Since cash and valuables are not permitted inside the prisons, purchases inside the jail are made using coupons. At the time of a mulaqat, relatives are allowed to give an inmate coupons worth 500 rupees. The coupons, in various denominations, allow the inmates to buy essential items such as tea, soap and buckets.

The ban on currency notes has given rise to a sort of black market inside the jail. If someone manages to smuggle a 500-rupee note, referred to as a gandhi, he can buy coupons worth 750 rupees. But the rate changes from day to day depending upon the number of 500-rupee notes in circulation on that day.

The gandhis are put to a variety of uses. They can grease palms and procure prohibited items like tobacco, drugs and alcohol, among other things. Tobacco is a contraband item in the jail; so smuggling cigarettes and pouches of tobacco is most lucrative. A pouch of tobacco costing twenty rupees in the market can sell for up to 400 rupees. A single bidi costs thirty rupees inside Tihar.

That evening a munshi came calling out my name and asked me to accompany him to the deodhi. He told me that my wife had come and led me to the mulaqat room. It was 4.00 p.m., the time generally meant for mulaqat of high-security inmates. Three other prisoners were already in the mulaqat room. It had been only few days since I had seen Aanisa, but it felt like a lifetime. After I was told by the social welfare officer that she too had been arrested, I was resigned to seeing her only in my dreams. And not having anyone visit me at all.

I saw Aanisa. She was looking tired and pale. Her face was marked with lines of stress and anxiety. Seeing me in such circumstances must have been extremely hard on her. But just the sight of her face, the mix of relief and sorrow, hit me hard and I broke down, weeping inconsolably. This was the first time I had wept before her. She was shocked. She did not know what to do. Quickly, she pulled herself together, and forgetting all her worries and tensions she asked me what the matter was. It was extremely frustrating to talk to her through the barriers. And under the watchful eyes of my tormentors.

I took a few moments to regain my composure. Then I told her about the welcome I had received at the time of admission, and the continuous harassment I was subjected to inside the jail. Aanisa said nothing. I could clearly see that she felt helpless and miserable. I did not know whether I had done the right thing by telling her about my suffering. Her life outside was not without problems either. She herself had turned pariah in the neighbourhood. Almost all the neighbours except the family of one S.A. Naqvi had become strangers—they pretended not to know her. The propaganda in the media had scared the whole neighbourhood to such an extent that they did not allow even their children to mix with my four-year-old daughter, Abyaz. But Aanisa did not go into a detailed account of her predicament. She was besieged by my misery. She was just telling me how she had visited the jail every day for the last three days, but she had been sent right back without being given any reason, when the warder started calling out, 'Time up! Time up!' I turned to look at him incredulously. Surely half an hour was not over yet. But he was right. For a jail inmate, visits from a near and dear one always go by in the blink of an eye. During my stay in jail, I learned not to be surprised when the warder called 'Time up.' The mulaqat was over. Aanisa went away with a heavy heart, and I returned with a confused mind, thoughts of my dear wife and my little daughter crowding my head.

Poor Aanisa. She had never seen this part of Delhi. Just getting to the jail was difficult enough. On top of that the insolent and insulting behaviour of the jail staff that she had to contend with must have been very trying for her.

The mulaqat is held in a hall which has several small enclosures. Each enclosure has three-foot-high brick walls with grills and meshes going all the way up to the ceiling. The inmates are on one side and separating them from their loved ones are thick meshes and grills with about three feet of no man's land in between. Imagine 200 people in that confined, poorly ventilated space shouting at each other. The whirring sound of a few powerful exhaust fans adds to the noise. In the melee you can get only a hazy view of your visitors and barely hear or make yourself heard. Often there are highly emotional scenes. People simply can't control themselves; they weep bitterly. But there is no one to console them. Guards behind them keep yelling, 'Time up, time up,' and sometimes even beat or physically drag away the inmates who are a little tardy with their farewells. The experience is harrowing for both inmate and visitor. The mulaqat room could do with a little bit of modern technology and human sensitivity.

While it is never a privilege to live in the high-security ward of Tihar Jail, the compensation is that these prisoners have mulaqat in the evening as there are just a few visitors for them. Since I was still a high-security prisoner in the jail book, I had mulaqat during this period along with just two inmates of the high-security ward. I was grateful for small mercies.

Later that evening I was summoned to the office of the jail superintendent, A.K. Kaushal. Aanisa's visit had cheered me up somewhat and I was not prepared for the outburst I encountered in Kaushal's office. He questioned me about my conversation with Aanisa. I told him that I had described to her the torture meted out to me at the time of admission and the continued harassment. 'What do you think this is, a guest house where you will be treated like a sahib? Forget it. This is a jail!' he shouted harshly. He asked me how I was treated in the ward. I replied that though there was no torture, humiliation and harassment went on. Without further ado he dismissed me and sent me back to my barracks.

Immediately after she left the jail Aanisa contacted V.K. Ohri and told him what she had heard from me. He in turn informed my journalist friends about the goings-on in the jail. The next day three of my journalist friends rushed to Tihar Jail to register their protest with the jail superintendent. Later in the afternoon, some 200 journalists assembled at the Press Club and marched to the office of Sushma Swaraj, union minister for information and broadcasting. They were so angry that they barged into her room. The minister gave them a patient hearing and telephoned Ajay Agrawal, Director General (Prisons), in front of them and gave him a dressing down and directed him to ensure my safety and security in the jail.

Sushma Swaraj's call had a powerful impact on the jail administration. They had not expected such a stern reprimand from a union minister. Suddenly, the wards began to hum with activity. A frantic cleanliness drive began. Every inmate was asked to clean his surroundings. Some had to clean the toilets and wash the floors of their barracks and wards.

The word had spread. Ajay Agrawal was coming to the jail, specifically to see me, I was told by a munshi. Jail officials said that it was the first time that the DG had visited the jail to address the problem of a particular inmate. I was called to the deodhi in the evening. Ajay Agrawal and A.K. Kaushal were sitting in the latter's office. Agrawal straightaway asked me what the matter was. I told him about the welcome I was given at the time of my admission to the prison. I gave him all the details of the incident, including the names of the persons involved.

He plainly told me that I had committed a very serious offence by indulging in espionage; therefore I must have been subjected to the treatment reserved for anti-nationals during their stay at Tihar.

I explained the nature of my case to him. He seemed sympathetic and assured me that I would not be subjected to any further harassment. He also said that he would instruct the administration that in future no inmate should be tortured simply because he or she was alleged to have committed a particular offence. I do not know whether such instructions were ever issued.

On the same day, 22 June 2002, a stream of people, jail staff as well as convict munshis, started descending on me. Everybody was curious to know what had happened. I got fed up with repeating the story of torture at admission time. All of them sympathized with me. Who knows how sincere they were! Surprisingly, none of my tormentors, except one constable, came to see me. And he threatened me with dire consequences if I took the matter any further.

As for the authorities, they took action at once. They had the full details of the incident and yet they sent a false report to the union ministries of home and information and broadcasting. According to the report I was not beaten up at the deodhi but there was a scuffle with some prisoners in the ward. It said that as I entered the jail I had shouted 'Kashmir Zindabad', upon which some infuriated convicts had beaten me up. The jail administration had taken proper legal action against them, according to the report. Actually, they quickly found some scapegoats and, using my complaint as a handle, fixed some poor fellows who were not even present at the time of incident. One of them was seeking parole to see his ailing son. He was denied the same on this ground. I rued my complaint and decided not to register any grievance in future, regardless of the provocation.

I did not deliberately tell the DG about the harassment at the ward, for by that time I had discovered that the most important people in any prisoner's life are not the minister, not the court, not even the DG or the jail superintendent but the warder and the munshi. Suppose you are facing some problem in your ward or in the barracks, you have two options. Either you go through the elaborate procedure laid down in the prison manual and approach the jail superintendent or you simply keep the warder or munshi in good humour. If you try to follow the manual, the chances are your misery will be further compounded.

The other, and only, practical solution is to keep the concerned assistant superintendents, warders, munshis and barracks pradhans in good humour. Keep these people happy, the experienced inmates advise, if one wants to have a hassle-free existence in the jail. I too did not attempt to breach the system. I always tried to be nice to them, though I did not have the means to make them feel good. 'Achha karna' is the code for giving money. But there is no end to it, as no amount is large enough for them.

Tihar Jail, like any other jail in the country, is overcrowded. The Delhi Jail Manual provides for the appointment of convict officers from among the convicts. These convict officers are called munshis and sewadars. Appointments of munshis and sewadars is made by the superintendent. The duties of these people include patrolling inside the wards, maintaining discipline, counting prisoners and such other tasks as may be allotted to them by the jail authorities. However, in practice, these convicts have become a sort of extra-legal authority for ordinary prisoners.

Once while the inmates were doing hard labour, a sewadar beat a Bengali inmate, Zahid (name changed), for being lethargic at the construction site. Zahid had been sent to jail under the anti-vagrancy law. In a fit of rage, he hit the sewadar with a brick. The sewadar sustained a head injury and had to be rushed to the hospital. All hell broke loose. Zahid was immediately caught and tied to a chair at the chakkar. He was ruthlessly beaten up and sent to solitary confinement. A criminal case charging him with attempted murder was registered. He was thereafter considered a kasoori, one who is unruly and needs 'correction'.

Appointment as a convict officer is a privilege. But even among them there is a hierarchy. The munshis who are influential get better postings; others are sent to not-so-prized positions. The privileged ones become a part of jail administration and are therefore entitled to better food and sometimes money as well.

An illegal income racket is run through this network of munshis and sewadars who are in direct contact with the ordinary inmates. They are also used to inflict corporal punishment on so-called unruly prisoners.

Those who do not have the means to make the jail officials 'feel good' are sent to do langar (community kitchen) duty or to Central Jail No. 2 where the factories are located. I had an opportunity to visit the langar. The prisoners working in the langar are very hard-working. Even though the langar is used to cook meals for more than 2500 inmates a day, it is astonishingly clean. Postings to the langar and scavenging are the most despised postings. Scavenging is euphemistically called 'Tata Sumo Driving', as the trolley meant to collect the garbage is called a Tata Sumo. The person collects garbage from the part of jail assigned to him and takes the trolley to the garbage pit. There he has to sort the garbage into biodegradable and non-degradable and dump it in the respective pits.

Munshis and sewadars assist the warders and assistant superintendents to assess the conduct of a particular inmate, recommend lodging in a particular ward, and supply and permit inmates to keep prohibited articles. One of the most important functions of the munshis is to help the jail administration to present a rosy picture of the jail to all outside visitors. While being incarcerated is a misery shared by all inmates, these convict officers are a privileged lot since their level of comfort, whatever that may be, is higher than that of ordinary inmates.

■

A typical day at Tihar Jail starts at 5.30 a.m. when all the inmates are woken up and counted. Thereafter, the prisoners are made to assemble in a courtyard outside their barracks for a mandatory prayer. Immediately after the prayer, around 6.00 a.m., the munshis, pradhans and warders select a few of the undertrials to wash and clean the barracks and the toilets.

Then breakfast is served. Those inmates who have not been entrusted any work are allowed to wander around in the open areas for a couple of hours. During this time, that is from 8.00 a.m. till about 10.00 a.m., some classes are held in the Mulahiza ward. Attendance is compulsory. Actually these classes were started during Kiran Bedi's tenure and were part of her reforms programme. Her idea was to impart education and keep the inmates engaged in some fruitful activity. Now the classes are far from the spirit of the original concept.

I used to sit in the graduate class. There were no permanent teachers here. The inmates would stand up and share their own experiences. A car thief would lecture on the opening of car locks. An inmate accused of defaulting on loans would teach how to defraud banks. A swamiji, an undertrial in a rape case, was assigned to teach undergraduate classes. Instead of imparting some spiritual lessons, the swamiji would provide tips to those held under rape laws and ask his students, accused of similar crimes, to describe in graphic detail their experiences, much to the lascivious delight of the class.

Some of these lessons had their lighter moments. Once a car thief was boasting of his achievements when a newly admitted prisoner said that his car, a Honda City, had been stolen from Karol Bagh, in west Delhi.

'Was it a white car?' the teacher asked.

'Yes,' said the inmate enthusiastically.

'Was an Esteem also stolen on the same day from that locality?'

'Yes, yes.' The inmate was quite astonished.

'Well, sorry, but I sold both the cars for a lakh and a half!' declared the teacher casually. The student could not contain himself and rushed at the teacher. Before either came to any harm, they were separated.

I must confess that during my stay in Tihar Jail I learned a great deal about things that I would otherwise have been clueless about: pickpocketing and picking locks, to start with, thanks to some enthusiastic teachers who were eager to show off their skills. One day a pickpocket stood up looking very agitated. He was upset that in the strict hierarchy in prison society pickpockets have a very low standing. Those accused of murder, dacoity, cheating and fraud are at the top of the ladder, while thieves and pickpockets are right at the bottom.

'We are kalakaars,' he complained. 'Like musicians, singers and magicians, our profession too requires not just skill but a great deal of riyaz, of practice too. The only difference between them and us is that the profession we have chosen is not recognized by the law.' He sounded quite convincing and since I was curious about their methods I asked him if he would teach me his craft.

'You will have to meet our guruji for that,' he replied. The guruji was also in jail at that time. However he was lodged in Ward No. 5; so I never got to see him. But I picked up snippets of interesting information from my conversations with the numerous pickpockets who were with me in jail. Pickpockets usually operate in a group of ten or twelve persons, called a 'company'. It sometimes includes women. In jail parlance a pickpocket is called 'machine' and those who assist him, 'thaikbaz'. The place where the company meets at the end of the day to divide the booty is called the 'phool'.

Pickpockets are trained in the actual methods of picking a pocket, using razor blades and knives, and jumping off and on to moving vehicles. They follow a regular schedule, their most active and lucrative period being the first week of the month and between 7.00 a.m. and 10.00 a.m. and between 5.00 p.m. and 9.00 p.m. They are equally efficient in crowded places like buses, markets or the vicinity of banks and in the not-so-busy areas. Most of them appear extremely courteous or helpful when the victim is pushed or splattered with some dirt to distract him, while an accomplice is relieving him of his wallet. Their most effective weapon, like the magician's, is distraction. They know that a human being focusses only on one thing at a time and they exploit this weakness. Being trained to be observant, they can tell a potential victim merely by watching his expression, movements and mannerisms. Many of these facts I knew.

What I did not know was that pickpockets follow a definite code of conduct. The rules for joining the fraternity are very strict, and once an individual joins he cannot leave. Each group has its designated territory and there is no trespassing. A weekly off is mandatory; so they do not ply their trade on Tuesdays.

One of the oldest and most widespread crimes in the world, pickpocketing does not qualify as a major offence. If an individual is caught, the punishment he is given is neither long enough to reform him nor severe enough to act as a deterrent. One inmate told me that the police have of late taken to planting small amounts of smack on them to ensure they stay in jail longer.

Anil (name changed), a handsome but reticent young man, was adept at picking locks of any description—even the fancy ones which are number-coded. He enlightened me on the technique of opening locked cars to steal them. 'Every lock can be opened, whatever the safety features are, once its lever mechanism is understood,' he said.

'But what about cars fitted with a remote locking system and alarm?' I asked, puzzled.

'It is quite simple. The whole system runs on the car battery. We just push the indicator a bit and short-circuit the electric wiring. That is sufficient to make the alarm system go kaput,' he explained.

According to him the most secure safety feature for cars at the time was the satellite tracking system. However the system was not available in India. But Anil was confident that car thieves would have cracked the system by the time it came to India. 'R&D work on it is already going on,' he said.

Anil's was the classic story. He was an intelligent young man, a graduate who had tried hard and failed to get suitable employment. So when a friend introduced him to the trade he thought he would steal just as many cars as would fetch him enough money to start a business and then quit. But then, how much is enough? He has thirty cases pending against him for car theft in Delhi courts alone.

I was once called upon to act as a counsellor by one inmate. He had been booked for bigamy. He had been happily dividing his time between both women without either of them knowing of the other's existence. When eventually they did find out, both filed complaints against him. Whenever his bail application came up before court, both wives would reach there. First, they would abuse each other and then abuse this fellow jointly and vehemently oppose his bail plea. The court would simply adjourn the hearing.

Both the wives were asking him to leave the other wife if he wanted a withdrawal of complaint. He was perplexed. He could not possibly satisfy both of them.

When he explained his dilemma to me I advised him, 'Tell both your wives that you will live with the one who secures bail for you.'

The ploy worked. Both competed for his release. The man was released but I don't know what happened to him outside!

Satbir Singh Rathi was an ACP of the Delhi Police, accused of shooting two businessmen, Jagjit Singh and Pradeep Goyal, in cold blood. He was an MA and had done a diploma in human rights. In jail he was pursuing a Ph.D. in human rights. Satbir was considered an 'encounter specialist' while working with the police. Now he is going to be a human rights specialist.

The admission of a eunuch creates a huge problem for the jail authorities. Where should they lodge the new entrant—in the women's ward or in the male wards? The presence of a convict eunuch in the jail made matters easier for them. She could tell if the eunuch was predominantly male or female. Her diagnosis was later cross-checked medically. Anyway, life for a eunuch was miserable in the male wards especially in Ward

Nos. 5 and 6 of Jail No. 3. There were twenty-five to thirty eunuchs lodged in Tihar, accused of murder, extortion and soliciting for prostitution.

One day a group of young Sikhs labourers were sent to the Mulahiza ward. They had been working in Moscow, but had been deported to India via Dublin. While aboard the plane, these people planned to seek political asylum in Ireland. They formed a political group and asked for asylum in Dublin on the grounds that they feared persecution for their political views. At Dublin they were confined in an asylum home. Enquiries were made. The Government of India denied the existence of such a political group and stated categorically that the men were not wanted in India for any crime. The Irish authorities deported them to India after thirty-two days. To their consternation the Delhi Police were waiting to welcome them at the airport and escort them to Tihar Jail. They spent their time there blaming each other for their predicament.

Another unexpected presence in the jail was a venerable maulvi from a village in Haryana. He was inside for allegedly committing a fraud, that of performing an innovative Khatam-e-Sulaymani, that is invoking Prophet Suleiman (peace be upon him) to shoo away evil spirits who were supposedly haunting a young girl. He was paid 3000 rupees by the girl's father. After he performed the Khatam-e-Sulaymani the maulvi returned to his village. Some time later, when he was in Delhi, he thought he should pay a visit to the girl's father, believing him to be a follower of his. Unfortunately for the maulvi, the Khatam-e-Sulaymani had not worked and the girl's condition had remained unchanged. The girl's father, a famous criminal lawyer, had got the maulvi arrested for fraud. The poor maulvi found it very difficult to explain the real meaning of the Khatam-e-Sulaymani to the judge. The fellow was lodged at Tihar for four months before he was granted bail.

The Afghan national Ghulam Mehboob was a case of damned if you do and damned if you don't. He was denied an extension of refugee status by the United Nations Commission for Refugees on the grounds that the Taliban, at whose hands he feared persecution, had been decimated, and therefore he should return to his country. The man went on a hunger strike before the UN High Commission office in Jor Bagh, Delhi. He was arrested and sent to jail. Someone in jail advised him to write an application that he could not go back to Afghanistan as he was loyal to the earlier Taliban regime and feared persecution at the hands of current regime. His letter landed him in bigger trouble. The jail authorities shifted him to the Highlight ward fearing he was a fierce Taliban supporter. He was sentenced to one year in prison.

A source of great inconvenience for the jail administration was a contingent of twenty-eight blind people. The police had not recorded their names correctly, which created lots of problems in the jail. Once they went on a hunger strike en masse and said that they would not eat until the jail superintendent himself came and talked to them. The jail officials made a convict pose as the jail superintendent. These poor inmates narrated their woes to the convict in the belief that they were talking to the superintendent. The convict assured them that action on their complaints would be taken and persuaded them to break their fast. To me this was being deceitful, even if it was to get them to eat.

The jail had some unusual inmates as well. A colony of ducks lived in the small park inside the jail. A barracks was reserved for them as shelter at night. A convict sewadar was deputed to guard and look after them. They were counted every day before being set free in the morning and again when they were locked up. A careful account was also maintained of the eggs laid and ducklings hatched. The schedule of locking and unlocking the ducks was the same as that of the prisoners.

■

I was very depressed in the jail, not because of the terrible quality of the food, especially the tea, or the fact that we were woken up at 5.30 a.m., locked up after lunch at 10.00 a.m., released for a couple of hours at 3.00 p.m., and then locked up again after dinner at 6.00 p.m. My greatest grief was that I had nothing to read or facilities to write. I asked my lawyer to apply to the court to allow me library facilities. Since the library was in another ward, and inmates are not allowed to visit another ward without permission from the jail authorities, I had to get the necessary permission. Accordingly, my lawyer made an application before the court on 3 July 2002.

The court sought a report from the jail authorities. Upon receipt of the notice, the jail authorities allowed me to visit the library for one day and reported to the court that I had been already allowed to visit the library between 9.00 and 10.00 a.m. The next day when I wanted to go to the library, I was refused permission by the warder. This continued for the next ten to fifteen days. One day I saw Assistant Superintendent Thomas and told him that the warder was not allowing me to visit the library. He immediately called the warder and roundly scolded him.

The warder did not take this kindly. He had his revenge. He would allow me to visit the library but would always waste precious minutes before letting me enter. And then he threatened that if I returned even a single minute late he would hang me upside down. Thus I got only about twenty minutes in the library. Besides I was not allowed to borrow any books.

After that I requested my lawyer to request for directions from the court to jail authorities to shift me to Ward No. 11. The jail authorities replied, 'The accused wants to be lodged near library, which is a common place of movement. Such a location will help him to develop links and communications with other Kashmiri and Pakistani criminals in this jail. Prison administration cannot allow him to be in a situation where he succeeds in carrying out his evil design. His request may, therefore, be rejected forthwith.'

The report also mentioned that the ward I was lodged in was the best one for a first-timer and that I had been allowed to retain two books supplied by the family. Naturally the court believed the report and rejected my application for a shift to the Ward No. 11.

In fact nothing except clothes and fruits were allowed to me during the mulaqat. My wife had to send me books through the jail superintendent's office. They retained these books for weeks together in the name of censorship. Generally it took them at least a fortnight to vet the books. But I could never understand the parameters of the vetting. They disallowed Khushwant Singh's biography and Nelson Mandela's best-seller, *A Long Walk to Freedom.*

Later on I came to know that there were only three Kashmiris in Ward No. 11, and none of them were hardened criminals. There were many more Kashmiris and even a few Pakistani inmates in Ward No. 10, where I had been lodged.

I was really amused the facade of the 'concerns' shown by the jail administration for the welfare of a first-timer as well as their 'apprehension' about my 'evil design'.

It was also very disheartening that the court did not adequately consider my credibility as an accredited professional journalist. It simply believed the contentions of the jail authorities as if I was a 'criminal' or a dreaded 'terrorist' trying to hatch some conspiracy. It bodes ill for the future of the judiciary in the country if the courts take statements of the authorities at face value. The duty to unearth the truth skilfully concealed in the maze of bureaucratic jugglery is of utmost importance for a justice delivering system.

After almost a month in jail I was permitted to subscribe to a newspaper. I chose the *Indian Express*. A convict would distribute the newspapers at around 9.30 a.m. When I received my copy the very next day I was surprised to see only the two sports pages. When I asked the convict where the rest of the paper was he simply said the *Express* has reduced its pages to just two, and there was little I could do about it. In fact all other pages were censored as the *Indian Express* had carried an investigative story on the petrol pump scam.

Hindi newspapers were not as heavily censored. *Hind Samachar* was the only Urdu daily allowed in the jail. Once in September, it too was banned, till I told the jail superintendent that *Hind Samachar*, a publication of Punjab Kesri group, was actually a super-patriotic newspaper. Immediately before my release, I succeeded in getting a nod for the Urdu daily *Rastriya Sahara* as well.

One of the things I discovered while in jail was that misery breeds superstition. And incarceration is misery compounded by helplessness. During my early days in jail, I found it impossible to eat the food. And the quality of the tea was so bad I gave up drinking tea. Noticing this, one inmate said to me, 'Every prisoner has a fixed quota of jail food ordained by fate. Eat it up and finish it, then you will be out quickly.'

I wanted so much to believe him.

Since the Mulahiza ward was meant for first-timers, almost every day some inmates were released. Once no one was released for almost a week. The prisoners began to get restive. They began to look for omens. One of them spied a poor dark-skinned inmate who used to sleep near the door of the barracks. He was deemed the culprit. The Rihai ki devi (the goddess of release) was repelled by his ugly looks, they said in chorus. He was humiliated, punished and made to sleep in a dark corner of the barracks so that the goddess would not see his face. They also tied some green chillies and lemons above the gate to ward off evil spirits.

Sunday newspapers, which carry astrological forecasts, were popular in jail. Some inmates who had a smattering of palmistry were much sought after.

Before I knew it, it was August and Independence Day was celebrated with much gaiety. All the inmates were assembled at the chakkar. The occasion was a big morale booster for me as I saw many persons among the prisoners about whom I had read in the newspaper. Also all those who inhabited Jail No. 3. The national flag was hoisted and A.K. Kaushal took the salute presented by the jawans of the TSP. He then gave a speech emphasizing the importance of being in a free country. Who else but this audience would know better the meaning and significance of freedom! A special meal, consisting of greasy soybean and fried paranthas, was served that day.

On 17 August my name was struck off the rolls of the Mulahiza ward and I was sent to the IGNOU ward. Before I was admitted there I was weighed. I had lost 12 kilograms since my admission.

The IGNOU study centre was initially set up in one barracks of Ward No. 11, but following the overwhelming response of the inmates the whole of Ward No. 11 was reserved for realizing Kiran Bedi's concept of 'Reformation through education'. Later on a study centre of the National Open School was also started for imparting school education under the open learning system. According to the authorities, more than 800 inmate students are enrolled in various academic and professional courses. They had started with twenty-seven.

One barracks in the ward was converted into a library, another barracks houses the computer lab, commercial art and typing classes, while two barracks are reserved for classrooms. The computer lab had three obsolete machines donated by a reputed private company engaged in computer education in India and abroad. The social welfare officer told me that they donated computers not worth more than 50,000 rupees but got the administration to spend almost a lakh on publicity for their philanthropy.

During Kiran Bedi's time the inmates managed the study centre and no jail official was allowed to interfere. An old inmate, Atbir, who did his graduation and was enrolled in a postgraduation course told me how two former inmates, Shahabuddin Ghauri and Ghulam Nabi War, had nurtured the study centre with support from Kiran Bedi and Superintendent Tarsem Kumar. As Shahabuddin Ghauri was a research scholar from Jawaharlal Nehru University (JNU) he and Ghulam Nabi War had introduced weekly debates to recreate the atmosphere of a JNU hostel. The practice had continued till recently, I was told.

The IGNOU study centre has met the same fate as other reforms introduced by Kiran Bedi. It is a shadow of its past. Ample proof that in Tihar the individual matters, not the system. The blame rests squarely with the jail administration for allowing a good thing to degenerate. A semi-literate autorickshaw driver was entrusted with the job of principal. Only when a new assistant superintendent of the ward found he could not spell 'principal' was he removed from his post. The ward is a hub of many alleged swindlers, cheats and fraudsters.

In spite of all this the IGNOU ward is among the best in Tihar. It still serves as the face of Jail No. 3. Visitors are brought here to show how pleasant the environs of Tihar Jail are. Jail authorities would not dare to show any other ward to unsuspecting outsiders.

But visits by outsiders create a lot of problems for the inmates. They are made to clean and scrub the ward, wear clean clothes and put on an appearance of cheer all day just so that the authorities are shown in a good light. Once a delegation of foreign policemen and diplomats visited the jail as part of their training programme and they were impressed when they saw barracks fitted with television sets, the library, classrooms, computer room, art room etc. I told an assistant superintendent who was accompanying them that they should not paint such a rosy picture of the jail lest some people hearing about the comforts offered by it decide to descend here since conditions in their own country were quite difficult for ordinary citizens.

The IGNOU ward was meant only for those pursuing some course at IGNOU or the National Open School. But some highly educated inmates would seek admission in class 10 or 12 just so that they might be lodged here.

The library at the IGNOU ward was efficiently managed by an inmate, Atul Kohli. It had some books donated or rather, going by their condition, discarded by the Delhi Public Library. It had on its shelves antique books, old journals of the Institute for Defence Studies and Analyses (IDSA), books from the erstwhile Soviet Union and few books from the 1950s and 60s.

I was delighted when I laid my hands on six-decade-old issues of *Ranbir*, the first newspaper of Jammu and Kashmir, edited by the veteran journalist Lala Mulk Raj Saraf. The newspaper needs to be preserved on microfilms and kept in the major libraries of the country for the benefit of researchers.

Life at the IGNOU ward was comparatively relaxed. Unlike in other wards, prisoners were allowed to take their food inside the barracks and eat at whatever time they liked. Some prisoners formed groups, pooled their meals and ate together. But then, especially in winter, the food used to get cold. Also the dishes used to be tasteless, without spices and oil, as if one were on a boiled food diet. Though the jail canteen sold cooking oil, the inmates could not use the oil to fry dal or vegetables as the use of heaters was not allowed in the jail.

But there is much truth in the adage 'Necessity is the mother of invention'. The prisoners had devised ingenious ways of heating their food. They would use electric coils and make a heater out of them. The bathroom-cum-latrine inside the barracks was used as a kitchen to conceal it from the prying eyes of jail officials. Beside this heater, IGNOU and NOS study materials were also used to heat the meal. Since matches and lighters are also prohibited items in the jail, igniting the paper was an elaborate exercise. Electrical wiring used to light the bulb in the small temple inside the barracks was sparked to burn the paper. A person like me who kept books for reading had to guard them round the clock. Those who were not fortunate enough to get papers or books used plastic buckets or mugs provided by jail administration for bathrooms and latrines. Even dried chapattis served as fuel! Food received during mulaqat was not allowed inside the wards. However some prisoners managed to get the food into the ward after paying hefty bribes. That used to be a treat for all their friends.

One warder who used to come around 5.30 a.m. to open locks could count only up to ten. So instead of doing a head count he would go inside the barracks and make a physical check, scouring all corners, bathrooms and latrines to make sure no one was inside. Once Ibu Tombey, an inmate from Manipur, wanted to have some fun at the warder's expense. He rolled up his bedding to make it look as if somebody was still sleeping and waited for the warder to come round. As expected, the warder went inside for physical verification, saw the bedding, and thinking somebody was still sleeping, marched towards it and started to kick and abuse the bedroll. When the inmates burst into loud laughter, instead of realizing his folly and enjoying the joke, he roundly abused them.

Because I had enrolled myself for the IGNOU course in creative writing as well as in the certificate course in commercial art of the Industrial Training Institute, I was eligible to gain entry into this privileged ward. Besides, the hostility of jail administration had also died down.

Attending the classes at the study centre reinforced my perception of the superficiality of the reform programme. The prisoners called our commercial art teacher, Pradeep Kumar, a 'cartoon'. He used to reach the jail at around 12 noon though the classes started at 3.00 p.m. I was impressed by his commitment to the students until I was told that he came early so that he could have his lunch at the jail. He too got the special meals prepared at the langar for the jail employees.

Pradeep's style of teaching was comical. A typical class would start with him sending two students to fetch some roasted gram.

He would fill all his pockets and start teaching the class as he ate the gram, one by one. When his pocket became empty, the class was over. He started teaching our batch how to draw the English alphabets on a graph paper and then colour them as he had illustrated on the blackboard. Some days later he asked us to show him what we had drawn. He took one look at my sheet and declared, 'You can never learn art. You have spoiled the sheet. Get lost and don't come to me till you set it right.'

The next day, instead of drawing the alphabets afresh, I showed him the same sheet. He was all praise and asked other students to emulate me!

'Now there is a ray of hope,' he said, with a smile.

The course was for three months but in between the teacher was away. However when the three months were up, the jail administration announced that we had learned enough and started enrolling the next batch.

In spite of this teacher, the commercial art class has produced excellent artists. Lama and Ashok are superb artists and their paintings adorn the precincts of Tihar. Their paintings were presented as souvenirs to visiting dignitaries like Chief Minister Sheila Dixit and the noted Bollywood music director Bappi Lahiri. I had the opportunity to see both Ashok and Lama at work. They are amazingly deft and create beautiful paintings with a few simple strokes of the brush.

Another equally committed teacher from the Industrial Training Institute, Pusa taught typing. He was a strict disciplinarian and an 'intellectual'. He expected his students to be alert and attentive at all times. He wrote an article entitled 'Tihar Ek Sapna' (Tihar: A Dream) on the comforts and facilities available to the inmates at Tihar in the in-house newsletter. The inmates who did not appreciate his autocratic manner prayed that his dream would be realized and he too could have a taste of the 'comforts of Tihar'.

Among the successes of the IGNOU study centre at Tihar was a convict who graduated from IGNOU and was appointed as an accountant in the university after he had served his sentence. Another undertrial prisoner, Vinod, facing charges under Section 302 of the Indian Penal Code for murder, was granted bail five years ago for a sum of 25,000 rupees. But his family could not afford to arrange the sureties to bail him out. It proved a boon for him. Vijay had come to jail as an illiterate, but he studied hard throughout his stay. Today he is a commerce graduate. The trial in his case is over and he is anxiously awaiting the court verdict. Hopefully, he will be able to start his life afresh.

IGNOU courses also had proper exams, but the conduct of examinations at the ward was a revelation. Copying was rampant as nobody from IGNOU generally comes to supervise the examinations. Some well-connected 'students' were able to send answer sheets outside the examination hall, where they were completed and returned.

Once I was deputed to be an invigilator. I forbade copying and did not allow answer sheets to leave the hall. The students pleaded that nobody would pass the examination. One senior student argued that the study centre had been established to provide necessary qualifications to the prisoners so that they might get some jobs outside and did not return to the crime. Studying in jail conditions was not a joke, since there was no proper faculty. Therefore students deserved some leniency. Another student said that I was unnecessarily harsh to them. In hindsight I guess they were right. The study centre was indeed a farce. The teachers from among the prisoners were paid a measly fifty rupees a month.

A complaint was made and I was relieved of my duties from the next day.

■

Kiran Bedi, the first woman to be recruited to the prestigious Indian Police Service, was sent to Tihar Jail as Inspector General, Prisons, on a punishment posting. But Bedi, known to be a daring officer willing to take on the world, took it up as a challenge and tried to introduce many reforms in the largest prison in the world. In her short stint of seven months, she managed to introduce certain changes which were in keeping with her concept of imprisonment and punitive action. Besides the reform through education, vocational training aimed at rehabilitation and Vipaasana and meditation practice, she also tried to improve the living conditions and the health care facilities in the prison.

However most of the reforms she undertook have not survived, especially in the hospital. The doctors still send one common medicine to all the patients, as if the tablet is the panacea for all ailments ranging from fever to stomach ache to cough and cold.

Once when some prisoners were heating the food on their electric heater under the TV stand, a jail official strolled along outside their barracks. The prisoners were in a fix. They could not bring out the heater, but if they did not take the dal off the fire, it would start burning and the smell would attract the attention of the warder. So they hit upon an idea. One of the inmates had recently been operated upon and still had some stitches on his chest. They told him to pretend he was in great pain and scream in agony so that the warder could be sent off to get medical help. The man performed the part extremely well, even feigning unconsciousness. Since he was supposed to be a heart patient the jail official rushed off to call a doctor. In the meanwhile the heater was turned off. A doctor arrived. Without asking a single question, he injected two medicines into the patient's hip from the other side of the grill and went away.

After a few minutes, he returned with an assistant superintendent. The doors were unlocked and the prisoner was taken to the jail hospital. For three days he was kept there and medicines were generously injected into his veins. He gaily abused his friends for making him suffer, all for the sake of some fried dal.

One day I too took ill and was hospitalized. I was given a bed with a mattress and a pillow. I had forgotten what it was like to sleep on a proper bed, and tossed and turned all night!

Later I got an acute stomach ache just before lock-up time. I sought permission from the warder to see the doctor. He allowed me to go to the hospital and told a sewadar to accompany me. The doctors, without even hearing me out or touching my stomach, gave some tablets. I returned with the medicine and took one tablet. At around 10.00 p.m. the pain in my stomach became worse. I started vomiting and nearly lost consciousness. My fellow inmates shouted for help. But it was half-an-hour before a jail official came. 'What is the problem?' he asked with volley of abuses.

'One guy is very sick,' someone replied.

'Who?'

'Gilani.'

He was furious. 'Let him die, the traitor,' he said and went away. (The man came to me a few days later and apologized saying he had mistaken me for the 'Parliamentwala Geelani'.)

The pain increased. My fellow inmates had no choice but to resume shouting for help. Then a warder came and sent a message to the hospital. A doctor appeared, saw me from the other side of the grills and gave the same tablet. I could not even tell him I had already taken the medicine. He too went away.

I again vomited the medicine. The pain was quite unbearable. My barracks mates were now extremely worried. Only a few months ago, somebody had died in the barracks in similar conditions. Shouting for help was the only thing they could do. So they started it again in chorus, their voices echoing their concern. Half an hour later a group of jail officials appeared. After the ritual abusing they asked what the matter was. An assistant superintendent was also with them. He ordered them to take me to the emergency ward. There were three other patients in the ward. Two patients were on artificial respiration.

In the morning a convict working in the hospital came and removed the oxygen mask from one of them and ordered him to clean the floor. After some time he returned and ordered the other patient on artificial respiration to clean the bathroom. Next came the milkman. Instead of distributing the milk to the patients, he placed the jug in the middle and told us to drink it up quickly. With just one plastic glass between the four of us— two suffering from tuberculosis—we obeyed his orders.

In the outpatient department of the jail hospital, where I happened to go several times, doctors hesitated to touch the prisoners. They did not even use stethoscopes. The dental surgeon in the jail hospital was the only exception. He treated his patients well and paid proper attention to them. At least he did to me when I went to him with a toothache.

One elderly inmate was familiar with most medicines since he used to run a medicine shop. Imagine his horror when he was given some tablets meant specially to subdue people suffering from schizophrenia. Some doctors routinely prescribed these drugs to anyone who came to consult them.

The death of Rajan Pillai, the famous businessman, in 1995 while in judicial custody created an uproar. It was alleged that he died because of lack of proper treatment in Tihar Central Jail. The Delhi Government appointed the Leila Seth Commission under Section 3 of the Inquiry Commissions Act, 1952 to enquire into the circumstances of his death. There are so many poor in this country who are suffering in the jails and die because proper medical treatment is not given to them. What of them? Who will answer for them? Will merely transferring an official help?

■

Kiran Bedi's efforts to bring about reforms in the prison system stemmed from her belief that a prison is an institution to correct people, not to punish them, for incarceration itself is a punishment that deprives prisoners of their liberty, choices and even clothes. If, along with this, they are subjected to more pain, prisoners may hurt society more once they go back to it. Therefore it is safer and wiser to change them while they are inside. She says, 'By not correcting them in jail you will be punishing society.'

The reforms that Bedi initiated at the Tihar Central Jail as Inspector General (Prisons) did help the prisoners during her tenure. Almost every day she would visit the barracks and interact with the inmates and this contributed in a large way to the success of her reforms. Unfortunately her idealism and dedication did not permeate into the rest of the jail administration. And after her departure, the programmes did continue but the spirit underlying it was nowhere to be seen.

In retrospect, Bedi's experiments in Tihar seem both simplistic and populist. Her programmes have not only missed the real issues but failed to address the social realities of an Indian prison. For example, she banned smoking inside the prison, even though there are many prisons in India where smoking is permitted. This gave the jail officials the easiest and most lucrative handle for illegal aggrandizement. Prisoners found ways to manufacture cigarettes in the jail itself using fine paper. I had to guard my English dictionary virtually round the clock as its fine paper was eminently suited for manufacturing cigarettes. The jail superintendent refused to distribute copies of the Holy Koran with English translation, donated to the prisoners, as the paper was of same fine quality. He feared that if inmates used the holy book to roll cigarettes, it could spark a bloody row as Tihar Jail has a very large percentage of Muslims.

Bedi's decision to prohibit non-vegetarian food in the prison too became another avenue for corrupt jail officials to mint money.

Bedi also introduced petition boxes to allow inmates to air their grievances. The complaint boxes, modelled like post boxes, are still seen hanging on the walls outside the deodhi and near the gates of every ward. The mobile petition box, called the DG's petition box, also remains in its place. But today no prisoner dares to drop a complaint in these boxes. This is because the DG's office sends all the petitions to the respective jail offices for action, and the prisoners have painfully learned that action is taken not on the complaint but on the one who makes it.

This is not to denigrate Bedi's efforts but no attempt at prison reform in India can succeed if it does not also deal with the attitudes and methods of other agencies directly involved, such as the police and jail officials, the medical staff and the social welfare officers.

Since I have no means to check the nuances of change that took place during Bedi's period, all I can say is that today Tihar Central Jail qualifies as one of the worst prisons in India. From my conversations with many inmates who had been around a bit, I learned that jails in Bareilly, Bangalore and Rohtak have far better conditions.

Today prejudice and punishment have a free run at Tihar. The maxim that prisoners are always guilty seems to be ingrained here. So regardless of who commits a mistake, the punishment is invariably reserved for the prisoners. To illustrate, one night, at around 10:30, the jail sirens started wailing. We were all shocked as it was not a common occurrence. A host of jail officials descended on the Mulahiza ward and all inmates were ordered out. A head count was undertaken several times. The inmates thought that there had been a jailbreak. It turned out though that the register showed one person more than the number of persons who should have been inside. Tempers were frayed and nerves were on edge. The hapless prisoners bore the brunt of frustration and anger. Finally around 4.00 a.m., the jail officials discovered that a double entry had been made while admitting the new entrants. One name was entered twice in the register: once the prisoner's own name and once his father's name. For no fault of his the poor fellow was badly beaten up.

The jail has its own intelligence system. It reminded me of the infamous Hari Ram Nai, the mole planted among the prisoners by the jailer in the Bollywood blockbuster *Sholay*. One did not know how many Hari Ram Nais were there among the inmates in Tihar. Once a warder was told by a Hari Ram that someone wearing spectacles had smuggled in some tobacco. The warder immediately acted on the information: all the inmates wearing spectacles were summoned and given a thorough thrashing.

The similarity with *Sholay* extended to the attitude of the jailors as well. They too declared like their screen counterpart, *'Hum angrezon ke zamane ke jailer hain, hum un logon mein se nahin jo qaidiyon ko sudharne ki fikr mein lage rahate hain, hum jaanate hain ki tum nahin sudhroge.'* (We are jailers of the British period; we are not from among the people who are busy trying to reform the prisoners, as we know for sure that you cannot be reformed.)

In fact one warder used to say in a typical filmi style, *'Mujhe sarkar ne power nahin di hai warna tumhe mar mar kar theek kar deta.'* (The government has not given me the authority; otherwise I would have beaten you all into shape.)

Wit was not lacking among the inmates. The martinet deputy superintendent V.D. Pushkarna was given the nickname Punishkarna Saheb.

The jail administration has devised ingenious ways of punishing the prisoners to keep them in place. The prisoners are frequently shifted from one ward to another. Originally this was put into practice to prevent the formation of criminal gangs, but now it is used as a form of punishment. Sending prisoners to another ward is called *'ginti katna'* (striking off the rolls). Sometimes these transfers lead to very touching scenes. Inmates often form deep relationships with each other and the thought that you may never see your companions again is very distressing. What makes it worse is that the transfers are sudden and swift, with no chance to say good-bye.

But it is equally true that there are frequent clashes among the prisoners. Many of them bear scars of these fights, inflicted by shaving blades and knives (improvised from spoons or any other flat utensil). Therefore barbers are under constant watch. The violence in the barracks, or more commonly during the bus journey to and from court, is triggered off by overcrowding or personal rivalries and jealousies.

The segregation of prisoners is a perfectly legitimate practice aimed at separating first-timers from hardened criminals. However, this practice too has degenerated into a form of punishment and degradation. An assistant superintendent segregates the new entrants, usually on the day after their admission, in the Mulahiza ward according to their alleged offences. This practice is a sort of humiliation session for the new entrants especially those charged with lighter offences like pick-pocketing, stealing etc. Strangely, those charged with murder, dacoity, robbery and other heinous crimes are spared. Prisoners charged with espionage or similar crimes are also subjected to severe punishments and humiliation, as my experience bears out.

Consigning prisoners to the High-Security Ward, called Highlight Ward in Tihar parlance, is a serious punishment, entailing solitary confinement. The High Security ward has its own 'kasoori cells'. Kasooris are provided meals only once a day. They are not provided with a fan. Ordinary prisoners dread being put in the solitary confinement as kasooris so much so that even a severe beating at the chakkar is preferred.

Long spells in the Highlight result in grave psychological damage to the inmate. Anybody who is shifted after a long spell in the High-Security ward to a general ward feels completely out of place and often implores the authorities to send him back to Highlight. Two such prisoners were shifted to the general ward for their good conduct after three years in the Highlight. One among them was chosen to participate in the annual Tihar Olympics as he was a good cricketer. But he could not bear to see so many humans and found the din of human voices intolerable. He begged to be sent back. He went to an assistant superintendent and offered him 5000 rupees to shift him back to Highlight. It was his misfortune that the jail official refused the bribe as he was an efficient officer who took his duties seriously.

Corruption among jail officials is a boon for prisoners seeking some small comforts. It is an open secret that any need can be fulfilled if one satiates the greed of the jail staff. All sections of jail administration, except the social welfare department, have openings for making a fast buck.

There is nothing subtle about the jail authorities' efforts at making money. The use of force to extort money is common. The prisoners' criminal records help them to identify the 'cows' whom they can milk. Very often, those involved in cheating and fraud cases are beaten and harassed till they agreed to cough up the amount the authorities demand.

Expectations of getting some money at a future date also have a mellowing effect on jail officials and convict munshis. I saw a prisoner literally enjoying his stay in the jail. He had been arrested for possession of fake currency. He had promised almost everybody rewards once he was out of jail.

The mulaqat room is one of the most lucrative spots in the jail. Payments promised to jail officials are made there by the relatives. Taking home-cooked food inside the jail can cost as much as 500 rupees. A fellow inmate, Amit (name changed), was accustomed to seeing an assistant superintendent take 100 rupees from his brother each time he came to visit. One day the official told him, 'Amit, I feel bad taking a hundred rupees from your brother every time.' What had occasioned this change of heart, wondered an astonished Amit. The official's next words dispelled any illusions Amit may have had about the man's attitude: 'Tell him to give me 500 rupees at one go so that he need not have to pay me again and again.'

The jail officials would stoop to any level, I realized, when one day a fire broke out in the dhobi's storeroom. All the inmates were told that the clothes they had given for washing or ironing had all been burnt. The next day we saw some warders wearing those very clothes.

■

Though the Delhi Jail Manual expressly prohibits the gathering of prisoners for the performance of religious functions, Kiran Bedi had demarcated places for mandirs and mosques in every ward to provide prisoners with a place where they could get spiritual solace.

While her intentions were certainly noble, in reality they were inherently biased in favour of the Hindu community. It is a fact that while the jail has a disproportionately high percentage of Muslims among the prisoners, there was not a single jail official who was a Muslim. It seems strange that for a community which forms around 12 per cent of the total population of the country, 30 per cent of the jail population is Muslim. Most of these Muslim inmates are inside for allegedly committing petty offences.

I must state here that during the holy month of Ramazan the atmosphere in the jail was quite amiable. The jail authorities helped the Muslim inmates to observe the fast. They provided them with sehri (the predawn meal) and the food was comparatively better than the meals on other days. But this cooperative attitude was absent on the Eid festival. While I was there, the Muslim inmates requested the jail authorities for some special food on Eid-ul-fitr. They were asked to collect money for the purpose, and told that the administration would provide milk for preparing the vermicelli, but they would have to forgo the weekly kheer. The Muslim inmates collected coupons worth more than 12,000 rupees to buy vermicelli and dry fruits. Imagine their surprise when they were served vermicelli boiled in plain water.

I was witness to a most shocking incident, bordering on open hostility to Islam, during my stay at the jail. One afternoon in September a convict munshi came with a list of prisoners and asked them to come out with their bag and baggage. Almost all of them were Muslim. My name too was on the list. We were told to march towards the chakkar to be lodged in Ward No. 5. All of us begged him to let us stay in the ward as we were pursuing courses from IGNOU. Some of us were also teaching the inmates. Another inmate was pursuing a master's in business administration, the only student from the entire Tihar community enrolled in the programme. But the munshi paid no heed to our pleadings. He had definite orders.

As we were proceeding towards the chakkar, Assistant Superintendent Rajendra Kumar saw me in the party and persuaded the deputy superintendent to allow me to stay in the IGNOU ward as I was his most disciplined prisoner. So I was sent back to the IGNOU while the rest of the prisoners were marched to Ward No. 5.

The reason for this sudden reshuffling was revealed a few days later. One day the gates were unlocked at 5.30 a.m. as usual, but immediately all inmates were rushed back into their barracks. Nobody knew what had happened. Some speculated that a war had broken out between India and Pakistan. All the inmates remained locked the entire day. The following day we found that two small open mosques in Ward Nos. 10 and 11 had been demolished. The 'mosques' were actually open platforms, without any roof, with a small almirah where copies of the Holy Koran were kept. The wall facing Mecca was given the shape of a mehrab, the dome typical to Muslim architectural.

The explanation offered by the authorities was ingenious. They told the inmates that they had found some improvised knives buried under the mosque. It was unconceivable how such items could have been buried under the mosque without damaging the cemented floor.

A number of temples dot the roads inside Tihar. Besides, there is big Hanuman Temple inside the Jail No. 3.

While the existence of places of worship offer some hope for the reformation of the prisoners, the same cannot be said about the self-styled religious preachers visiting the jail. While visits to temples and the mosques were voluntary, the jail administration had to use force to make the prisoners listen to the sermons of these preachers. Many of them were highly despised by the inmates because of their arrogance and self-righteous airs. These preachers treated all the inmates like hardened criminals and considered themselves sent by god to correct and reform them. They invariably exhorted the inmates to join their sect whenever they were out of the jail.

The only exception I found was Father Paddy Meagher of Vidhyajyoti College of Theology. He never indulged in sermonizing and was interested in listening to what the inmates had to say. He counselled them without burdening them with theological interpretations. Many inmates, especially foreigners, were quite attached to him.

Another person who was respected by almost everyone was the leader of the Vipaasana (meditation) programme, S.N. Goenka, who had a deep understanding of the prison situation. Since meditation was completely non-religious, it attracted inmates of all the religions.

Kiran Bedi had initiated a project to involve the community in her ambitious reform work. About twenty-nine non-governmental organizations are said to be participating in the programme, but during my incarceration I saw very few of them. I recall two Muslim bodies among the NGOs involved in the reformation programme. The Tableeghi Jamaat was the only Muslim organization to visit the jail. They too had the same self-righteous arrogance. They were ridiculed by the inmates since the allegory and metaphor used by them were simply bizarre. Their visits stopped after the mosques in our ward were dismantled.

No one from the other Muslim organization turned up during my stay in the jail. Their annual report published in Tihar literature mentions a number of their activities inside the jail, including details of a lecture programme aimed at convincing the inmates about the incompatibility of terrorism with the teachings of Islam. Did this organization really think that the Muslims inside Tihar were terrorists?

Many Hindu religious organizations regularly visited the jail. Members of the Sahaja Yoga, Aasa Ram Bapu Ashram and Brahmakumaris were regular visitors. The jail administration, though corrupt and insensitive most of the times, used to turn religious when these preachers arrived. Many practices adopted by these groups were alien to the simple Hindu inmates, so they refused to participate in those rituals.

A women social worker used to visit the prison on behalf of an NGO. She had a strange way of imparting legal advice to newly admitted inmates. She would visit them carrying a copy of the Indian Penal Code, look at their admission tickets, glance over the provisions of the relevant section and then inform the individual, in a mighty authoritative tone, what sentence he could be awarded. This frightened many inmates.

■

The jail officials have created a set of rules, which all inmates are expected to observe meticulously. This unwritten code of conduct was as follows:

1 The inmates shall not use cups to drink tea.
2 The inmates shall not sit on a chair; they can sit only on a stool.
3 The inmates shall always walk in queues along the side of the road and not in the middle.
4 The inmates shall stop whenever they see a jail official approaching and shall not resume walking till he goes away.
5 The inmates shall stand with folded hands while talking to any jail official and shall always address him as 'Sir'.
6 While visiting any jail official, the inmates will leave their footwear outside the room.

Anyone breaking any of the above, even by mistake, would come in for drastic punishment. I once saw a prisoner thrashed at the deodhi because he had dared to drink water out of a cup when he was on duty there. He did not have the steel glass mandated for prisoners for drinking water. Another inmate, usually absent-minded, addressed a jail official as 'Chacha' (uncle), for which he was beaten mercilessly as he had presumed to equate himself with high authority by addressing him as uncle! I also remember seeing an inmate punished for remaining seated on a bench outside the deodhi when a doctor happened to pass by.

Despite all the initial harassment during the later part of my incarceration I was spared some of the indignities reserved for prisoners. Two jail superintendents, Kaushal and Meena, treated me with respect. But they too did not dare to break the taboos imposed on the inmates. So they devised a novel way to circumvent them. Whenever I was summoned to their office they would leave their chairs and walk around as they talked to me.

Some of these rules had been discarded during Bedi's time but had returned to haunt the prisoners once again.

One day I was summoned by the semi-literate librarian, who had replaced Atul Kohli, and told to prepare a list of books since the jail library had received a grant of 30,000 rupees. I prepared a comprehensive list with law books, novels, jail diaries of leaders and books for those pursuing IGNOU courses in it. The list also included a jail manual and some books on civil liberties including rights of prisoners.

The librarian submitted the list to the assistant superintendent without even glancing at it. He boasted that he had prepared it. The assistant superintendent was furious. He couldn't imagine including books on prison laws and prisoners' rights. The poor librarian's wish to be considered an intellectual backfired on him. But he was an old hand and knew how to extricate himself from the situation. He fell at the assistant superintendent's feet and begged for mercy. Quickly he confessed that the author of that 'mischievous' list was Gilani.

By that time I had got wind of the developments. When I was summoned by the assistant superintendent, I explained to him that I was not aware of the rules which did not permit books on prison laws inside the jail. His reaction was surprising. He smiled and said that he knew all along that the librarian could not have compiled the list and sent me back.

The books never reached the library.

Five
Twists and Turns

If an individual gets caught in the labyrinthine world of secret security services, law enforcement and justice, he will find it extremely difficult to get out of it unless he finds a happy coincidence of support, solidarity and a stroke of luck. My journey to liberty was just such a difficult expedition, fraught with twists and turns, never easy, never predictable, with hope giving way to despair and despair sprouting fresh hope.

As I was led to the Special Cell of the Delhi Police at Lodhi Colony, I thought that it would be a matter of a few hours before I was back home. I had done nothing wrong, my entire life was above board, and in spite of ransacking my whole house the Intelligence Bureau sleuths had not been able to find anything to charge me with. No criminal case could be made out against me on the basis of the document recovered from my computer. And even if they tried to concoct a case against me it would be thrown out by the court, I was sure. I would try to convince my prosecutors that I was innocent. And hope good sense would prevail.

But my confidence was totally misplaced. I had not taken into account the evil machinations of the IB officers who came to raid my house. I had underestimated their power and reach. As was evident even during the raid. The Delhi Police officers were under pressure from my persecutors, who had the power to mislead the whole establishment, including the minister of home affairs, L.K. Advani. The way the judicial proceedings progressed also dealt a severe blow to my faith in the efficacy of the judicial system.

Right from my first appearance in court I felt I had little chance. I had told the Chief Metropolitan Magistrate, Sangita Sehgal Dhingra, that the document recovered from my computer was a published document. But my statement was not recorded.

The reply filed by the prosecution on 18 June said, 'Internet has been thoroughly surfed but the information contained in the documents mentioned above was not available on the Internet.' The reply, opposing my release, further said that a letter requesting verification of the source of information had also been sent to the ministry of external affairs through the ministry of home affairs.

Interestingly the urgency with which the opinion of the DGMI was obtained was not visible in securing verification of the source of published version. No verification had been filed till the conclusion of proceedings against me.

My friends looked for the original copy of the *Islamabad Papers* in various governmental and university libraries where the journal was regularly available. They found copies of all other issues of the journal, but this particular issue was missing. It was listed in the index of books and magazines but had vanished from the shelves. The authorities there said the issue was taken out of the shelves only a day before.

Fortunately my friend Jal Khambatta managed to contact Dr Shireen M. Mazari, director general of the Institute of Strategic Studies, Islamabad and requested her to send him a copy of this particular issue of the *Islamabad Papers*. Dr Mazari initially expressed her inability to provide the original copy of the issue since it was an old issue, dated 1996, and said she could send a photocopy of the issue from the archives since the institute had only a few copies.

When Khambatta explained why it was so important for the original to be presented, she graciously wrote, 'We managed to locate an extra original copy of the *Islamabad Papers*. We are sending it to you by courier. I hope this would help you in your proceedings.' The printed copy was received on 21 June 2002, and the same produced in the court.

I had read articles by Dr Shireen M. Mazari in some Indian periodicals, but I did not know her personally. Nor was she known to Khambatta and yet the kind of help she offered proved crucial to the process that ultimately led to my honourable release. I thank Dr Mazari for her help.

On 24 June 2002 my counsel placed before the court some additional facts giving another specific location on the Internet, www.defencejournal.com/2002/january, where the information was available. The prosecution also filed a reply to my bail application. It reproduced almost verbatim the claims made in the reply to my application of 15 June 2002 seeking my release.

On 2 July 2002 my counsel moved an application seeking the opinion of the DGMI taking the published version of the document into consideration. My counsel also offered to show the information on the Internet since the prosecution had claimed that they had surfed the Internet thoroughly and not found it.

The prosecution filed a reply to the application on 8 July 2002. The CMM rejected my application seeking a second opinion of the DGMI after taking into consideration the fact that the same information was published in 1996. Giving reasons for the rejection, the order said:

It is well settled proposition of law that investigation is to be carried out by the prosecution without interference. The information on the document in question has been obtained from the authority concerned. As per the opinion of the Directorate General Military Operations, the same has been found to be a document relating to a matter disclosure of which is likely to affect the sovereignty and integrity of India. The concerned authorities has also opined that *the information* has serious ramifications and *appears to have been compiled by an agent specifically tasked to observe and report the strength and location of troops.*

In short, the arguments of the defence counsel is that the document is not a secret document. This proposition has been laid to rest in Ram Swaroop V. State of Delhi 1986 Crl.L.J.526 (at 537) wherein it has been held that even if an information which may not be secret but is useful to the enemy or an unfriendly power falls within the definition of Section 3 of the Official Secrets Act. (Emphasis added.)

The reasoning given by the CMM was contradictory and misleading. It is a well-settled proposition of law that the courts have ample powers to meet the ends of justice. The courts need not wait to assume their role of justice dispensation till the prosecution fabricates a case against an innocent person.

When the court said that 'concerned authorities has also opined that the information has serious ramifications and appears to have been compiled by an agent specifically tasked to observe and report the strength and location of troops', it had all the more reason to order a second opinion on the document.

I had placed on record the published version of the document proving that the information contained in the document was not collected by me. This was sufficient to rubbish the whole opinion put forward by the prosecution to justify the case against me.

Besides, the court cited the Delhi High Court ruling in the case of Rama Swaroop to reject my application that publication of a document does not materially affect the prosecution case against me. The reasoning provided by the Delhi High Court in Criminal Writ 40/2000 in the matter of *Dr Narayan Waman Nerurkar V. State* (Through CBI) in its order dated 30 May 2001 is quite relevant in this connection. According to the decision the real test of applicability of Section 3 of the OS Act is to see whether the information relates to a matter the disclosure of which is likely to affect the sovereignty and integrity of India, the security of the State or friendly relations with foreign State or useful to an enemy.

If viewed in totality, this was not applicable in my case. The prosecution admitted that I was working as a professional journalist. The prosecution had not been able to provide even an iota of evidence linking me to the offence. The only legal evidence against me was the opinion of the DGMO which had been proved wrong by producing a published version of the document. The court should have exercised caution in taking the opinion at its face value. And my modest demand from the court was to direct a second opinion from the same authority taking into consideration the published version.

The unanimous resolution adopted by the Press Council of India, a statutory body established under an Act of Parliament as a protector of press freedom, declared categorically that citing the Ram Swaroop case was not applicable in my case. The council, chaired by a retired judge of the Supreme Court, did not have powers to take up my case since it was sub judice. However, in its meeting on 19 July 2002 held at Varanasi under the chairmanship of Justice K. Jayachandra Reddy, the council held that 'any information which is publicly displayed on the Internet cannot be treated as confidential and the reproduction or possession of such matter may not attract provisions of the Official Secrets Act'

My counsel Ohri had produced the Press Council resolution to Sangita Dhingra Sehgal, the CMM. But the order did not even mention the resolution. Ironically, Sehgal is now the secretary to the Press Council of India and will have to act upon the same resolution pertaining to the OS Act. The resolution of the Press Council of India is also part of the memorandum presented by about fifty Members of Parliament to the deputy prime minister. The memorandum says:

> To prevent the misuse of the Official Secrets Act the Press Council of India has suggested an amendment to Section 5 of the Act so that 'nothing shall be an offence under this section if it predominantly and substantially subserves public interest unless the communication or use of "official secret" is made for the benefit of any foreign power or is in any manner prejudicial to the safety of the State.' On the other hand, the Venkatachalaiah Commission on the Working of the Constitution has recommended greater judicial accountability in case of patently wrong judicial orders which grievously affect the freedom of the citizens. We request you to introduce both these amendments to the existing legislation at the earliest so as to uphold the Rule and Law and strengthen the credibility of the Judiciary.

Among the signatories to the memorandum were Justice Ranganath Misra, Fali S. Nariman, R.K. Anand, Kapil Sibal, Eduardo Faleiro, Dr Raja Ramanna, Pritish Nandy, Kuldip Nayar, Prof. Saifuddin Soz, K. Natwar Singh, Dr Biplab Das Gupta and Dr A.R. Kidwai.

The prosecution had disputed my counsel's statement that the document was available on the Internet. My counsel maintained that it was and pressed for showing the document on the Internet to the court. A journalist friend always carried a laptop to the court in the hope that my counsel would succeed.

The police produced evidence that they had surfed the Internet at a cyber cafe. According to the prosecution they had surfed on 31 July 2002 and had not found the website www.issi.org.pk. However, the evidence itself was not credible as the document they submitted could well have been produced by disconnecting from the Internet in which case it would say the document does not exist.

Many IB officials too used to visit the court to report progress in the case to their superiors. These IB officials once laughed at the journalists' innocence in believing that the website could be shown to the court. They knew they had blocked it using their clout.

What they did not know was that my friends had broken the 'apple' wall put to block the website and it was available on the Internet. It was a pity that my counsel could not persuade the court to see the existence of the document on the Internet. The judge once agreed to see if the document in fact existed on the Internet despite the repeated denials by the prosecution. A laptop was brought to the chamber where she was holding the in-camera proceedings. But when permission was sought to use her official phone line to connect to the Internet, she refused. Without that connection there was no way one could surf the Internet.

That the judicial process in India is slow is well known. But how slow I found out when my bail application filed on 18 June 2002 was disposed of on 13 November 2002. In the meantime the prosecution had filed the charge sheet. All the evidence the prosecution could piece together was before the court. The arguments on the application had also taken into consideration the 'evidence'.

The court rejected my application for release on bail. The facts cited for rejection of the bail application were contrary to the records available with the court.

In the order, after recording the rival contentions, the court noted that 'the prosecution has sent the document containing the "information" to the Ministry of External Affairs for verifying the source of the information and there is no doubt that the prosecution has taken too long to verify the same as it is still awaited even after five months since the accused was arrested'.

This was indeed a severe indictment of the prosecution as after production of the published version of the document, verification of source was a vital requirement.

Still, the court, instead of taking the indictment of the prosecution to its logical conclusion by granting me bail, relied on the arguments led by the prosecution.

Discussing the case against me, the order said:

Gilani has been arrested U/s 3/9 of Official Secrets Act and from the reading of Sec. 3 it appears that even an information which may not be secret but which relates to a matter, the disclosure of which is likely to affect the sovereignty and integrity of India, the security of state and friendly relation with foreign state or useful to the enemy is an offence U/s 3 of the Official Secrets Act. 1986 CRI.L.J. 526 Rama Swaroop V/s State. . .

14   During the course of investigation the document / 'information' was sent to the Army Authorities for expert

opinion. As per the opinion of the DGMO the information contained in the file is vital and sensitive relating to defence matters not originated by the army and compiled by an agent specifically tasked to observe and report the strength and location of the Indian Troops having serious ramifications of operational plan in J&K, besides being the 'information' directly useful to the adversary. There is a categorical opinion that the 'information' containing in the document is directly related to the defence matters of India.

15   Investigations revealed that e-mail directing Gilani to follow the *Mobility of Lone Sahib who was later on murdered* have been found during investigation. E-mails received and sent by the accused reflect that *he has an inclination towards liberation of Kashmir* which include e-mails giving details of the civilians of Pakistan who were trained by ISI of Pakistan for conducting Terrorist Activities in India and were killed in encounter by Indian Forces. (Emphasis added.)

16   One e-mail showing the stay of accused arranged at Hotel Mughal Sheraton, Agra was arranged by Pakistan High Commission. When verified it was revealed that Gilani had enjoyed his stay in Mughal Sheraton on the expenses of Govt. of Pakistan during the visit of General Musharraf to India. Gilani has also been found to have close ties with one Ghulam Mohd Bhatt, Deputy Chief Awareness Bureau presently detained under Public Safety Act.

17   Under Section 3(2) of Official Secrets Act it is not necessary to show that accused person was guilty of any particular act tending to show a purpose prejudicial to the safety or interests of the State. Prima facie the circumstances, conduct is enough to draw a presumption against the person so accused.

18   To my mind prima facie the case falls within the purview
      of Official Secrets Act which is punishable with a maximum
      imprisonment of 14 years. Keeping in view the larger
      interest of public and State and all surrounding circumstances
      there is hardly any justification for grant of bail.

The order failed to address the issue that simple possession
is not an offence. As a bare reading of the law makes it clear, to
put an act into the ambit of offence under OS Act, it must have
been done 'for any purpose prejudicial to the safety or interests
of the State'

In my case since the document was on record, the court
committed a grave mistake by not going into the contents of
the document in the context of my profession.

Further, in the light of the court's observation that the
prosecution had not been able to verify the source of information
after being provided with the published version of the document,
the expert opinion of the DGMO had become irrelevant.

The e-mail that allegedly directed me to 'follow the mobility
of Lone Sahib who was later on murdered' was purely in the
nature of professional advice. The e-mail was sent to me by
Nusrat Javed, senior journalist with the *News*. Javed had advised
me to follow 'the thoughts and mobility of Abdul Ghani Lone
and Yaseen Malik'. The full text of the e-mail was available in
the charge sheet, but the order shows a partial and selective
reading of it. It would also ensure continuation of my detention
even if I was freed in the OS Act case.

Again, the e-mail containing details of Pakistani civilians
killed in Kashmir was actually a criticism of Pakistan and
included in the memorandum submitted to the United Nations
Commission for Human Rights against the Pakistan government

by Abdul Hamid Khan, chairman of the Balwaristan Liberation Front.

Regarding the charge that I enjoyed the hospitality of the government of Pakistan, the evidence gathered by the police and available in the charge sheet contradicts the allegation casually made by the prosecution. Also there was no evidence to show that I had 'close ties' with Ghulam Mohammad Bhatt. And Bhatt was not under detention under the Public Safety Act at that time. He had already been released.

It is also pertinent to mention here that the Public Safety Act is not a punitive legislation providing punishment for committing some crime but it is a law providing for preventive detention. There was nothing to warrant a 'prima facie' finding against me about the applicability of the Section 3 of the OS Act. Neither the circumstances nor my conduct called for any such inference. And still the court refused the grant of bail.

But I was not the only victim of miscarriage of justice. A great number of the inmates in Tihar Jail were caught in the web of doctored police investigations and lapses in the administration of justice. Most undertrials were in jail for petty offences. As K.F. Rustomji, former Inspector General of Police and former member of the Police Commission wrote in the *PUCL Bulletin* (November 1981), 'The number of criminal repeaters in India is rather small. The number of dangerous criminals—psychopathic killers, murderers, professional robbers, burglars and compulsive rapists—would be very few.'

Soli Sorabjee, Attorney General of India, said in 2003, 'Criminal justice system is on the verge of collapse. Because justice is not dispensed speedily, people have come to believe that there is no such thing as justice in Courts...Hamlet's lament about the law's delays still haunts us in India and the horrendous arrears of cases in courts is a disgraceful blot on our legal system, especially the criminal justice delivery system...The gravity of this development cannot be underestimated. Justice delayed will not only be justice denied, it will be the Rule of Law destroyed.'

Many innocent people inside Tihar Jail were proof of this collapse.

Though in theory the law provides for anticipatory bail, in practice it is anticipatory punishment which abounds. An overwhelming majority of the prisoners in Tihar Jail were undertrials. Even the jail officials admit that more than 60 per cent of the prisoners lodged there are innocents. In some cases many prisoners spent more years in jail than they would have had they been convicted. According to People's Union for Civil Liberties, a study conducted at Bangalore prisons showed that half of those tried were acquitted, and of those convicted 75 per cent were sentenced for less than six months each, and only 6.4 per cent were sentenced to more than one year's imprisonment.

Data presented to Parliament in December 2002 is revealing. According to a statement by the home ministry, the total capacity of 1259 jails spread over India is 221,937 while the number of prisoners lodged therein is 289,013. Out of those only 72,304 are convicted while 216,709 are undertrials.

According to a study conducted by the National Commission of Human Rights 97.3 per cent prisoners in the Mulahiza wards at Tihar were undertrials. The findings also pointed out that 94.83 per cent of the inmates at the jails in Dadra and Nagar Haveli, 93.99 per cent in Manipur, 89.9 per cent in Jammu and Kashmir, 82.08 per cent in Nagaland, and 79.53 per cent in Karnataka were undertrials. The lowest percentage of undertrials was found to be in Tamil Nadu, where only 32.78 per cent of the inmates were undertrials.

Most of those languishing in jail were poor and unable to have themselves bailed out, unlike the privileged who have resources to escape the reach of the law even if they are caught. I saw a Nepali boy at the Mulahiza ward. He was there for almost a year. He had been granted bail by the court, but there was nobody to stand surety for him. The court had asked him to furnish a personal bond for 25,000 rupees which was reduced to 10,000 rupees and then to 5000 rupees. But he couldn't even come up with 5000 rupees.

A poor rickshaw-puller had to spend six months in jail for stealing 100 rupees. The man wanted to plead guilty to the charge so that he could get out of jail. However there was no one to plead on his behalf. Finally the in-charge at the judicial lock-up prepared his application, the man pleaded guilty before the court and was released since he had already undergone sentence.

The Delhi High Court Judge J.D. Kapoor in his order on 27 November 2002 expressed concern over streams of bail petitions pouring into the high court. The judge noted that while the Supreme Court has laid down clear guidelines for granting bail, the subordinate courts are increasingly refusing bail even in minor and less serious offences.

Paucity of judicial officers is one of the most important factors causing inordinate delays in dispensing justice. The Law Commission had recommended in 1987 a nearly fivefold increase in the judge–population ratio within five years but the government has still not implemented the recommendation. In fact even the vacancies in the judiciary are not being filled up promptly. The situation in subordinate judiciary is worse. What with 1874 posts out of a meagre 13,000 posts remaining vacant, almost 30 million cases are pending in the courts.

Low financial allocation is another issue plaguing the administration of justice. In India just 0.73 per cent of the total revenue is spent on the judiciary as compared to other countries such as the United Kingdom and Japan where it is 12 and 15 per cent respectively. The Supreme Court has directed that at least 10 per cent increase should be made every year. According to the direction almost 38,000 posts of judicial officers need to be created in the next three years. Owing to the work load, trial courts are finding it difficult to realize the directions of higher courts for time-bound completion of trials.

Examples of such delays are inmates like Amit Ratra, a young prisoner, charged with abetting robbery, and acquitted after seven years, and Mohammad Aslam booked under NDPS Act, whose trial should have been concluded within three months of 17 October 2002 as per a high court directive, but who was still languishing in jail.

In the case of one Vishnu, booked under the OS Act, the court had recorded evidence of all the witnesses except the investigation officer way back in July 2001. However, till my release from jail, the investigating officer had not been examined and poor Vishnu was still behind bars.

From all the stories I heard in Tihar, I was shocked to learn that it was extremely easy for an ordinary individual to be picked up by the police and thrown into jail indefinitely. One only had to bruise the ego of a police constable and he could fabricate a case against you, as Venu, from Kerala, discovered to his horror. He had come to Delhi to take an exam for a job. After the test he was strolling down to Buddha Jayanti Park when he was accosted by a policeman. The policeman could not understand English, and Venu did not understand his Hindi. Venu was booked for stealing 52 kilograms of iron grills valued at 600 rupees which the policeman allegedly recovered from his bag. It took Venu ten months to be granted bail and then several more before he got out on a personal bond.

■

But I digress. To come back to my story: on 14 June 2002, my friend Aunohita of the *Times of India* persuaded many journalists to sign a memorandum in my support, urging the government 'to ensure that the investigation is fair and judicious and that Gilani does not face any harassment or ill-treatment at the hands of the authorities'. More than 300 journalists signed the petition presented to the internal security minister, I.D. Swami. The memorandum wanted the police to make public all facts of the case and the charges against me.

On 20 June 2002 the Editors Guild of India sought a fair and open trial for me. A statement issued by the president of the guild, Hariji Singh, said that the charge against Gilani was that he possessed a 'published document' of the Pakistan government. The guild viewed the case of Gilani very seriously, Singh added. If he was detained indefinitely without trial, it would amount to curtailing the freedom a journalist enjoyed in a democracy. He demanded that the government make all the incriminating evidence against me public in the interest of transparency and warned that refusal to do so would force the public 'to draw the inference of a witch-hunt'.

On 6 July 2002 a delegation of the Delhi Union of Journalists (DUJ), a professional-cum-trade union body comprising the majority of journalists in Delhi, met the minister of home affairs, L.K. Advani, at his residence to plead for the withdrawal of the case against me and to raise the issue of victimization of other journalists.

Jal Khambatta said he would speak in my defence and prove my innocence.

The DUJ told Advani that it was preposterous to accuse me of going around personally to gather information for the benefit of Pakistan. They assured him that he was being misled by his intelligence agencies. They also presented to him the printed booklet containing the data found on my computer on the military deployment in Jammu and Kashmir and pointed out that the booklet published by the Institute of Strategic Studies, Islamabad was not banned. Khambatta informed him that the said booklet was available in many government libraries and in fact was in the possession of the senior BJP leader K.R. Malkani.

Even at the risk of getting arrested, Khambatta told Advani, 'I, too, have acquired a copy of the same information. If it is so dangerous that its possession was sufficient to warrant Gilani's arrest under the OS Act, then I should also be arrested.'

S.K. Pande, the DUJ president, requested Advani to look into the ongoing intimidation of journalists. He also urged him to have a sympathetic look at my case. However all that the delegation got was an assurance that Advani would examine the case and do the 'needful'.

On 20 August 2002, the DUJ petitioned the President of India, Dr A.P.J. Abdul Kalam, for my release. The President's office forwarded the DUJ petition to the home ministry for consideration. The petition was lost in the wilderness of the home ministry's estate.

Scores of journalists in groups had been calling on Advani time and again. He assured many of them that my bail plea would not be opposed, but nothing came of it.

Two journalist friends had been prevailing upon senior BJP officials for help. They were assured that I would get bail at the next hearing. However it was the same every 'next date of hearing'. The prosecution continued to oppose the bail tooth and nail.

In the meantime, Aanisa had gone to Srinagar to attend my younger sister's wedding. There she met Dr Farooq Abdullah, then chief minister of Jammu and Kashmir, along with my journalist friends Shujat Bukhari and Masood Hussain. Dr Abdullah assured her that he would take up the issue with the Centre. He deputed one senior officer of the state government to continuously monitor and report the progress in the matter to him.

Earlier my father, Syed Mohammad Masood Gilani, had also appealed to the President, the prime minister and the deputy prime minister seeking my release on the eve of my sister's marriage on 25 August 2002.

His plea said, 'I am a father with a bleeding heart. My son Iftikhar has been languishing in Tihar Jail since 9 June. As a father, I am constrained to join hundreds of his fraternity in appealing to the President, the Prime Minister and the Deputy Prime Minister for his release on the eve of the marriage of his sister.'

Still, I could not attend my younger sister's wedding.

The statutory limit of ninety days for filing the charge sheet was fast approaching. The police had moved the home ministry more than a month ago for the sanction to prosecute me but the sanction was withheld all these weeks. Non-filing of charge sheet would have entitled me to bail. During this time, an IB agent told me in jail that the government had granted sanction to prosecute me under the law. He also said that the charge sheet would be filed in time.

He turned out to be right. The charge sheet was filed on 7 September 2002. It was the last date for filing the charge sheet as per the date of arrest in the police records. If the charge sheet had not been filed within the stipulated period of ninety days, I would have been entitled to be released on bail under section 167 of the code of criminal procedure. My hopes were dashed. A pall of gloom engulfed me.

I began to feel that perhaps all assurances were hollow. I was in for a long haul. If the government really wanted me to get bail, just a few days' delay in filing the charge sheet would have been enough.

In the end filing the charge sheet came as both a blow and a boon. Withholding the charge sheet would have given the unscrupulous elements an opportunity to fabricate evidence and level some more serious charges. Now the whole matter was crystal clear. The whole 'iceberg' was exposed. And it was smaller than the proverbial tip in size.

The charge sheet filed in the court by the Delhi Police said:

On the basis of investigation conducted so far, the seizures made, the opinion obtained, scrutiny of e-mails and bank accounts of the accused and the statements of the prosecution witnesses, there has been sufficient evidence on the file to Charge Sheet the accused, Syed Iftikhar Gilani U/s 3 and 9 of the Official Secrets Act 1923 R/W 120-B and 292 IPC.

Detailing the circumstances of registration of the criminal case, the charge sheet said that on 9 June 2002 investigating officer Inspector Raman Lamba had been called to my residence by ACP Rajbir Singh, where Deputy Director of Income Tax Saurabh Kumar handed over a complaint to him along with a five-page printed document extracted from my computer. The charge sheet said that the computer file of the document was 'Forces' with a heading 'for reference, strictly not for publication', and it contained details of the strength of the army and paramilitary forces in Jammu and Kashmir.

According to the charge sheet, the document was found to be violative of Section 3 of the Official Secrets Act, 1923. Therefore a case was registered against me. The document was sent to the Director General of Military Intelligence of the Union Ministry of Defence for opinion. Section 9 of the OS Act and section 120-B of the Indian Penal Code (IPC) were added later on.

The charge sheet further alleged that in the garb of a press reporter I was conducting espionage in India and was supplying information about the strength of the army and paramilitary forces to Pakistan.

In addition, the charge sheet recorded the seizure of eleven pornographic video compact discs (VCDs) from me. I was accused of being a sexual pervert: 'the hard disk of the computer of the accused was perused and it was found that there are several e-mails indicating that the accused is involved in or inclined towards group sex. Therefore section 292 of IPC has been added.'

The charge sheet accused me of being a supporter of the liberation of Kashmir and cited as proof the existence of an e-mail entitled 'Atrocities of Forces in Gilgit' containing 'details of alleged atrocities of Pakistani forces and the Inter Services Intelligence in Gilgit area of Pakistan Administered Kashmir'. It had details of civilians from Pakistan who were trained by the Inter Services Intelligence of Pakistan (ISI) to conduct terrorist activities in India and were killed in encounters by Indian forces. The charge sheet says that I enjoyed a stay at the Hotel Mughal Sheraton at Agra courtesy the government of Pakistan.

The charge sheet said that I was directed through an e-mail to follow the 'mobility of Lone Sahib', who has since been killed.

It was further alleged that I had indulged in financial transactions and investments amounting to more than two million rupees, which according to the charge sheet were 'unexplained'.

■

Aanisa was always optimistic, telling me at each and every meeting that I would be released soon. Our friends too kept boosting her confidence. She had been knocking at every door to get whatever help she could. But I had stopped believing her.

In the meantime, my friends approached any Member of Parliament who would listen to them. Those who supported my case were Dr Raghuvansh Prasad Singh (Rashtriya Janata Dal), Ramjilal Suman (Samajwadi Party), Hannan Mollah (Communist Party of India-Marxist) and Eduardo Faleiro and Suresh Pachori (both Congress).

Once during the regular briefing of the Congress its spokesman Anand Sharma too demanded a fair trial for me. Cutting across parties, various leaders of Jammu and Kashmir, including Ghulam Rasool Kar, Prof. Saifuddin Soz, Abdul Raheed Shaheen and Yusuf Tarigami supported my innocence. Ghulam Rasool Kar, Prof. Saifuddin Soz and Abdul Raheed Shaheen even visited my house to show solidarity. Abdul Raheed Shaheen raised the issue in the meetings of the Parliamentary Standing Committee of the ministry of information and broadcasting.

The Politburo of the Communist Party of India (Marxist) issued a statement demanding my unconditional release.

Now elections in Jammu and Kashmir were over and Mufti Mohammad Sayeed had assumed the chief ministerial position.

Even before coming to power, he and his daughter Mehbooba Mufti had pledged their support to me. Sayeed took up the issue of my continued detention with the central government in his very first meeting. Thereafter, the issue remained a permanent item on his agenda in every meeting with the Home Minister L.K. Advani.

During the campaign among political leaders some of my friends came across some very disturbing weaknesses in our democratic system. Even parliamentarians claimed helplessness, though one of them, Dr Raghuvansh Prasad Singh, raised the issue in the Lok Sabha.

'Gilani' had become a dirty word with so many Gilanis painted as villains. Senior parliamentarians too had confused me with S.A.R Geelani of the Parliament House Attack case.

My wife was my only source of contact with the outside world. She kept me informed of developments during our meetings in the court and during her visits to Tihar Jail twice a week. She seldom missed the days on which she could have a mulaqat.

On one such visit, I advised Aanisa to meet the former president of the Samata Party, Jaya Jaitley.

Aanisa called Jaya Jaitley, who invited her to her residence for a meeting. Jaitley was quite moved after hearing the full story. She took up my case with then Defence Minister George Fernandes, and a few days later George, as he is popularly known, asked Aanisa to meet him.

She was given a warm reception at his residence. She had not imagined that someone occupying such a high position in the government would entertain the wife of a person accused of the most serious offence under the OS Act, and that too with so much patience and cordiality. George assured her with paternal affection that she should not worry any longer. He invited her to shift with our children to his house if she felt threatened at our home. He said he would try and visit me in jail.

My journalist friends had not given up their efforts. They kept pestering Advani for my release whenever he interacted with the media.

On 30 October Aanisa moved an application to the Defence Minister George Fernandes urging a review of the adverse opinion given by the army authorities. She stated that the opinion rendered by the DGMO on 14 June 2002 was erroneous, since it had not taken the published version of the document into account. The application urged him to institute an enquiry into the matter.

The defence minister took up the matter with the DGMI and also contacted Advani, now the deputy prime minister.

Hopes were raised in December 2002 as I had moved for interim bail to celebrate Eid as well as the birthday of my three-year-old son, Mujadid. However, it was not to be. I was denied bail. Jaya Jaitley learned about the birthday and insisted that Aanisa should celebrate it. She went with some friends to my house and spent a couple of hours there. I was overwhelmed.

The DGMI ordered the examination of the printed document and ensured that the opinion rejecting the earlier assessment reached the Police Commissioner of Delhi before the next hearing.

A Sessions Court had already asked Delhi Police to secure a fresh opinion of the military. Instead of approaching the DGMI, as the prosecution had done in the first instance to secure the first opinion, this time it approached the home ministry. But the earlier opinion was repeated verbatim.

However, the following day when my counsel produced the original opinion of the DGMI, the judge summoned the DGMI and the Joint Commissioner of Police to settle the issue. The DGMI attended the court and explained the matter.

The home ministry mandarins panicked at this development, as it was a matter of grave embarrassment for them.

Ultimately, the home ministry rejected the DGMI opinion, and simultaneously issued separate orders to the Lt Governor of Delhi for withdrawal of the case. The arrangement was conveyed to just one person handling my case and that too in strict confidence. They were not to tell my wife, my lawyer or me about it.

Accordingly B.R. Dhiman, Under Secretary (Internal Security), appeared before the court and informed the judge about the rejection of the DGMI opinion and reaffirmed that the government still considered me guilty of the offence under the OS Act.

The CMM again summoned the DGMI and the Joint Commissioner of Police on 13 January to settle the issue. Within an hour of the adjournment of the case, the home ministry rushed the file to Lt Governor Vijay Kapur for withdrawal of the case.

The Lt Governor signed the order for withdrawal of the case and the prosecution was ordered to get the release order issued by the CMM by approaching her at her residence since it happened to be a holiday for the court. However, the CMM was out and could not be approached throughout the day.

The next day, a Friday, the prosecution moved the CMM's court for withdrawal of the case but she put the same for the date already fixed.

The Delhi Secretariat had functioned till late in the night on Wednesday, 8 January 2003 to complete the formalities and issue the withdrawal order.

The government wanted that the media should know about my release on the day after my release, after I had already spent a night at home. The news of the government moving the court for withdrawal of the case was out and journalists besieged my wife. There was virtually a stampede of journalists in my house, everyone wanting to interview Aanisa and other family members.

Aanisa chose to spend the next day away from home. On Monday morning, she had a really tough time getting to the court. The whole area was swarming with electronic and print media crews. She had to cover her face with a shawl and leave the maid to answer questions.

George Fernandes had not only helped immensely in restoring my freedom but also sought to give a healing touch after my release. He invited my family and me to spend some time with him on Republic Day. He cancelled his attendance at the President's reception just to spend time talking to me before I left for Jammu to personally thank everybody at the *Kashmir Times*.

He organized yet another dinner to which he invited my family along with the retiring DGMI, Lt Gen. Lohchab, and his wife. After the DGMI left, George spent hours telling me to put the pain and the anguish I had suffered behind me and look forward to a bright future.

Six The Role of the Media

I never thought that I would be the subject of the great deconstruction and reconstruction of the maxim 'The pen is mightier than the sword'. But I learned during my incarceration at Tihar that the pen is a double-edged sword.

I have been through an unfortunate experience. But through it all I have also realized how fortunate I am. Fortunate for several reasons. Because I was based in Delhi, I had a reasonably large circle of friends among the journalist fraternity. My friends knew me well, as well as they knew the system. They were fully aware of how some sections of the media are manipulated by some governmental agencies. And that the powerful fourth pillar of democracy was not a monolith where generalizations could not be made.

I was fortunate that the *Kashmir Times* was my employer. Our chairman, Ved Bhasin, had enough faith in me to vow to defend me with all his might. An appeal issued by the *Kashmir Times* stated, 'This is a conspiracy to tarnish his image and to put curbs on the freedom of the press. We are hoping for support from the journalist fraternity worldwide and expect them to express solidarity for Iftikhar and rally behind us in our protest against his arrest in a totally fabricated case.' They started a campaign called 'The Truth behind Iftikhar Gilani's Arrest' to expose the false case foisted on me.

Ved Bhasin visited me and my family. He rushed my editor, Prabodh Jamwal, and executive editor, Anuradha Bhasin Jamwal, to Delhi. Prabodh Jamwal addressed a press conference in Delhi, along with Aanisa, on 14 June 2002 and publicly vouched for my innocence. Those were difficult days. Not many people were prepared to take this stand so openly. At great risk to himself, Jamwal released the published version of the document that the government had been describing as a secret defence document.

My friends knew that reports filed by my colleagues were not out of malice or bias. And unless my side of the story was forcefully presented, it would be very difficult for some of them to change their perception. And they were right. Very soon most journalists reporting on my case realized the game plan of some interested sections of the government and solidly put their might behind me.

I am proud to be a part of such a fraternity, who steadfastly questioned the canard spread by some vested elements. I take pride in the fact that my fraternity, being part of the fourth pillar of democracy, took a stand where many prominent members of the first pillar, Parliament, faltered.

Outside the high prison walls, journalists worked for my release, cutting across all barriers, ideological or otherwise. Some took active positions; others worked privately. But I learned much later that almost all national dailies carried detailed reports rubbishing the prosecution case against me.

The Delhi Union of Journalists was the first to react to my arrest. The DUJ organized at least three protest rallies. Its president, S.K. Pande, rushed to the Press Council of India and led a delegation to plead with the Deputy Prime Minister L.K. Advani that my arrest was an attack on the freedom of the press and that I should be released at once. He also mobilized other journalist organizations.

The Editor's Guild too registered its protest. Its president, Hariji Singh, and other member including editors Dilip Padgaonkar, M.J. Akbar and Sumit Chakravarty too pursued my case with the government.

Many international bodies, notably the Committee to Protect Journalists (CPJ) based in New York and Reporters Sans Frontieres (RSF) based in Paris and the International Federation of Journalists (IFJ) based in Brussels, took up the issue with the Government of India. The CPJ even urged the US Secretary of State Colin Powell to take up the matter with the Indian government.

S.K. Pande was a great support to Aanisa. He attended the court hearings and every time there was a possibility of my being released on bail, he offered himself as surety. He also deputed two DUJ activists, Jal Khambatta and Umakant Lakhera, to coordinate with my lawyer for any assistance he might require. Khambatta and Umakant rushed to Tihar Jail, along with another journalist, Dharmanand P. Kamat, to take up the issue of my torture at Tihar with the jail superintendent.

M.K. Venu, another journalist, worked actively at an individual level. Like Pande, he too offered to stand surety for me. Neither Pande nor Venu knew me personally and yet they were willing to vouch for me. Their gesture means so much to me. The support and the faith shown in me by all those journalists who hardly knew me and yet stood up for me gave me the strength to survive my incarceration.

The report by Asha Khosa, the first journalist to proclaim my innocence, made the *Indian Express* remark, amid the din of propaganda, that in my case the authorities were 'skating on thin ice'.

Speaking at a felicitation hosted by the Press Club of India on my release, Vinod Sharma, chief of bureau of the *Hindustan Times*, said, 'For the first time, after Rajiv Gandhi's Defamation Bill, 1985, have journalists united over a cause and succeeded in making the political leadership of the country see reason and end the farce.'

I did not know most of the journalists in Srinagar personally. My only contact with them was through my writings. But their response was overwhelming. On 10 June 2002, as soon as they heard of my arrest, they thronged the streets and demanded a fair investigation and my release. Sitting elsewhere in India, one cannot imagine the risk involved in conducting a protest march in Srinagar. But braving all risks, the entire press corps of eighty journalists marched to Raj Bhavan. Led by veteran journalists Yusuf Jameel, Nizamuddin Bhat and Ahmed Ali Fayaz, they met Governor Girish Chandra Saxena and asked him to intervene in the matter. They approached almost every central and state leader and pleaded my innocence even though they did not know me personally. Their confidence in my innocence was a tremendous morale booster for me.

Tarun Vijay symbolized the blurring of ideological lines. His position as the editor of the *Panchjanya*, the Hindi organ of the Rashtriya Swayamsevak Sangh (RSS), did not come in his way of supporting me. Just a few weeks after my arrest when the propaganda was at its peak, he brought hope to my father and my wife. He told them that the gloomy period would soon be over as he knew that I was innocent. He knocked on L.K. Advani's doors many times. Whenever Aanisa went to meet him in his office at Jhandewalan, he received her with courtesy and respect.

Somewhere between these moments of pride my heart goes out to those poor souls who I saw rotting behind bars in Tihar.

They were not so fortunate as to have their version presented to the public through the press. Many of them had not done anything wrong. But they did not belong to the fraternity I belong to, nor did they have friends among them. There was none to plead on their behalf. But it is equally true that the miseries of many of them had been compounded by acts of commission and omission of my own fraternity. The poor unfortunates did not know whether my colleagues were a boon or a bane.

In the course of our daily rounds of reporting and commenting, perhaps we tend to forget the more basic emotions and sentiments. We need to relax for a while and think about the implications of our reports. We must ask ourselves whether in the mad rush of catching deadlines, headlines and bylines, we have committed a gross violation of natural justice, whether the report filed by us would in effect amount to condemnation of some innocent person without affording him an opportunity to present his side of the story.

One morning as we were being herded to attend the court date, an assistant superintendent, Jitendra Kumar, told a subordinate that there were orders to take me to the court in chains. I tried to tell him that there was no such court order. But insistence and protest have no meaning in a prison. I was sent to the chakkar to be fettered. The official responsible for putting a prisoner in fetters had not come. In the interim I tried my best to get the officials there to see reason.

Luckily, a deputy superintendent arrived and asked what was going on. The officials told him they had been ordered to put me in shackles. I mustered enough courage to tell the deputy superintendent that there were no court orders and the prison officials had been mistaken. He asked for my warrant and satisfied himself that there was indeed no such order. Immediately he demanded an explanation from the concerned assistant superintendent. The assistant superintendent claimed to have read a news report that stated that the court had rejected my application not to be fettered during court proceedings. The assistant superintendent was given his due by his boss.

The next day I came to know that a Hindi newspaper had published a news item confusing me with S.A.R. Geelani. The reporter had not bothered to differentiate our two cases.

But the mother of all mischievous reports was that of a crime reporter of a leading English daily. She reported that I had admitted to having ISI links. The report said, 'Iftikhar Gilani, 35-year-old son-in-law of Hurriyat hardliner Syed Ali Shah Geelani, is believed to have admitted in a city court that he was an agent of Pakistan's spy agency.' The report appeared in the paper on 11 June, a day after I was produced in court for the first time for seeking police remand.

Although the paper's court correspondent had correctly reported the day's proceedings, the crime reporter must have been offered an 'exclusive' after the daily police briefing and it did not occur to her to cross-check the story with the paper's court correspondent. One of the more fanciful quotes attributed to me was 'My father-in-law was so impressed by my motivation and dedication to the cause of jehad that he married his daughter to me.' Quoting officials who had interrogated me she reported that I had confessed to knowing many ISI agents, with whom I was in regular touch. At that time I had not even been questioned by either the IB or by the Delhi Police. This was clearly an example of irresponsible reporting. It came in handy for a section of the IB to confuse the journalist fraternity.

All Delhi papers usually reach Srinagar in the afternoon. However, on 11 June 2002 the newspaper carrying this mischievous report was rushed to Srinagar in the wee hours and circulated among key journalists, who were spearheading the campaign for my release and fair investigation.

The report put a damper on their mission. They thought that everything was lost since I had allegedly confessed before the court. The highly respected columnist and legal expert A. G. Noorani was so agitated by this report that he called my wife and Ved Bhasin from Mumbai and told them to immediately counter the deliberate misinformation. Even the Delhi Police officials at the Special Cell were disturbed by this report. They wanted to know if I knew the crime reporter and had talked to her. I denied having anything to do with her.

Perturbed by the report, Aanisa contacted the deputy chairperson of the paper. She was given a patient hearing and treated with utmost respect. Realizing the damage the report had caused, the deputy chairperson ensured that the paper published a denial and a complete version of the story.

Though the paper made amends, there were many who had read the first report and not the denial; so the needle of suspicion continued to hang over me for months together.

On 10 June 2002 a headline in a Hindi daily read 'Huge amounts of wealth and some sensitive documents recovered from house of the son-in-law of Geelani during Income Tax raids'. The report carried on in a similar vein. The next day the same newspaper reported 'Gilani's visitors used to come in expensive cars', and cast serious aspersions on my integrity. Another report on 12 June in the same daily said I was in constant touch with international Islamic terrorist organizations. The newspaper attributed many false statements to people in my neighbourhood. That I worked in my study till the wee hours of the morning was held against me, as if it was not the bane of every journalist filing his stories from home.

My friends approached the editor to bring the untrue reports to her notice. She said that she had tons of information against me. However, she stopped the publication of such far-fetched stories when told that my friends would go to court on the issue.

Another leading English newspaper said:

'Iftikhar Ali Geelani, son-in-law of jailed Hurriyat leader Syed Ali Shah Geelani, was the Delhi-based point man of Mohammad Yusuf alias Syed Salahuddin, the Pakistan-based commander-in-chief of the terrorist outfit Hizb-ul-Mujahideen (HuM). Investigations by Delhi Police have revealed that Iftikhar used to provide advance information to Salahuddin about the moves of Indian security agencies. He had camouflaged his real motives behind his journalistic facade so well that it took years for security agencies to unmask him, well-placed sources said...

He overtly spoke against the Hurriyat amalgam and even wrote articles criticizing its leadership. It was a very cleverly worked-out ruse to hoodwink Intelligence and security agencies...

He misused the freedom and access which is provided to newspersons here. It took the agencies long to pounce on him as he enjoyed the protective cover of an accredited correspondent.

On 11 June 2002 a Hindi paper published a photograph of my wife coming out of the Special Cell after meeting me. But the headline of the story proclaimed 'Iftikhar arrested, wife Aanisa absconding'.

Almost all papers carried reports on the recovery of a laptop from my house. I have never owned a laptop. In fact even the police never claimed to have confiscated a laptop from my house. But no one seemed to have questioned these planted stories—how else would they have believed that I was resident editor of two Pakistani newspapers, the *Nation* and the *Friday Times*. It is not possible to be a resident editor of a Pakistani publication in India. When we have not even allowed foreign direct investment in the print media, appointment of a resident editor would mean the newspaper was published from India. And how can one person work for two rival publications published from the same place, that is, Lahore?

Dainik Jagran was the most popular daily in Tihar. I began to dread the time after class when the inmates would have got to read the sensational reportage of the *Dainik Jagran*. The warders, munshis and convicts would point to the news item about me and ask for an explanation, and then dismiss all I said as false and punish me. In fact I owed the torture I had to undergo on the day of my admission to the gross misreporting by the newspapers. Who would believe me when they could see it in black and white? For them the printed word, especially if printed in the *Dainik Jagran*, was the gospel truth.

If news reports were to be believed, I was in possession of vast quantities of foreign currency, was the owner of some Wall Media Productions, a three-bed-room flat which I had purchased for 13 lakh rupees, had amassed undisclosed income of 2.2 million rupees and had evaded income tax of 7.9 million rupees, and I regularly received huge funds into my accounts as well as in fictitious names. The appearance of such motivated news items compounded my misery.

Come to think of it, I must thank the media for informing me about the incriminating document found on my computer. It was when one of the raiding party members switched on the television that I first heard about it while the raid was going on in my house. Various news channels carried the news in their own versions. According to Aaj Tak, I was absconding from my house. For Zee, my wife was absconding. Doordarshan announced that I was being questioned. NDTV was quite reasonable. Aaj Tak flashed the news that some sensitive defence document was found on my laptop computer.

All the reporters were trying their best to get favourable quotes from neighbours and bystanders, anyone who would make their stories spicy. They managed to get hold of one of our former neighbours, Vandana, who now lives far away from us. She had come to the society to find out what was going on. The neighbours told the reporters that she would be able to give them authentic information about us. When a reporter asked her about us, Vandana replied that we had been the best neighbours she had ever had during her fourteen-year stay in Delhi. She was literally shooed away and told she was doing a disservice to the nation by siding with traitors.

Even after my release some of my gullible media friends, who had lapped up all the fanciful stories against me, once more fell for the bait and were persuaded to write that some fresh evidence had been found against me. The evidence was that I had visited the Pakistan High Commission fifty times, that I owned another flat in the posh Vasant Kunj area of Delhi and that I had received 'very high' foreign remittances. This story landed at the newsdesk of a prominent daily. The editor cross-checked it and then killed the story.

One fallout of my arrest and the negative publicity in the press was that the Press Information Bureau arbitrarily cancelled my accreditation. I read this news in the *Dainik Jagran* while in jail. However the Lok Sabha press committee under the chairmanship of V.P. Naik, bureau chief of the popular Marathi daily *Sakal*, stood by me and put the matter on hold.

Even my Lok Sabha accreditation which had been suspended was restored within a week after my release, thanks to the good offices of Abdul Rashid Shaheen, Member of Parliament, who spoke to Lok Sabha Speaker Manohar Joshi. The Speaker, despite being a member of the Shiv Sena, was sympathetic. But the Press Information Bureau took its own time giving me my accreditation back.

From my experience I have learned that a new approach and culture for crime reporting has to evolve. It is not fair to put cub reporters on the crime beat and then expect them to file interesting stories. If there is pressure on them they have no option but to befriend the police and hope to get scoops, exclusives or leaks. Of course they have to pay a price for this privilege, namely write whatever they are told to by the police or the investigating agencies. Since it is not always possible to get the victim's side of the story, it would help if the police gave out information that was factual rather than manipulated to project them in a good light. Some newspapers have taken the initiative in not publishing any 'leak' without getting a version from the other side. This needs to be adopted by other media establishments as well.

Here it might be in order to quote the sagacious advice of Rattan Mohan Lal, guru of Lala Mulk Raj Saraf, the father of journalism in Jammu and Kashmir. Lal had sent these wise words to Saraf on 1 July 1924 when he founded *Ranbir*, the first newspaper of Jammu and Kashmir. He said:

> I hasten to congratulate you on bringing out the *Ranbir*. The sturdy infant shall one day rise to full proportions of a highly developed institution and you cannot be too careful to bestow your undivided attention to this growth. Let your tone be serious rather than idealistic, practical rather than commonplace and sympathetic rather than hypercritical. But guard yourself against being too grave, pontifical and patriarchal. Infuse humour into your notes, make them light but not flippant. Be always on the side of law, order and constitutionalism. Let your style be vigorous not flamboyant, simple not jejune, direct not blunt. Let it strike a happy medium between the plain and the ornate. Do not use such words as sensational which is nonsense...Make a discriminating use of new terms of speech. Don't let passion get the better of your reason. You cannot cleanse the world of its evil by a stroke of the pen, however vigorous it may be. Remember to climb down from the cloud-land of ideals to hard facts. Never permit your criticism to be bitter or one-sided...I need not play the part of a preacher to you. Your qualifications, public spirit and the stern integrity of your motives shall make you equal to the exigencies of journalistic life.

No better advice seems possible.

Seven
The Law and Its Misuse

The OS Act, 1923 is a draconian law. It does not have any safeguard against its misuse. Being a relatively less used legislation, it had escaped the limelight so far. Now that there seems to be a spurt in cases under this law, the time has come for a serious review of it.

The charge sheet contained more than 225 pages of documents as evidence supporting the allegations levelled against me.

Before entering into an analysis of the evidence attached with the charge sheet, it would be appropriate to discuss the relevant provisions of the Official Secrets Act and the Indian Penal Code.

I was accused of violating Sections 3 and 9 of the OS Act, read with Section 120-B of the IPC. The section is not only vague in defining the offence but makes concessions to the prosecution as far as proving the offences in the court is concerned.

Section 3 of the OS Act maintains that a person can be detained if he, for any purpose prejudicial to the safety or interests of the State, approaches, inspects, passes over or is in the vicinity of, or enters, any prohibited place, or makes any sketch, plan, model, or note which is calculated to be or might be or is intended to be, directly or indirectly useful to an enemy, or obtains, collects, records or publishes or communicates to any other person, any secret official code or password, or any sketch, plan, model, article or note or other document or information which is calculated to be or might be or is intended to be, directly or indirectly, useful to an enemy, or which relates to a matter, the disclosure of which is likely to affect the sovereignty and integrity of India, the security of the State or friendly relations with foreign States.

The section further provides that if the offence has any connection with the defence matters of the country then the punishment may extend to fourteen years, while in other cases it may be up to three years.

The statute considerably reduces the burden on the prosecution to prove the charge in a court of law, since Section 3 provides that it shall not be necessary to show that the accused person was guilty of any particular act tending to show a purpose prejudicial to the safety or interests of the state.

The law dispenses with the necessity of proving any particular act against the accused, and states that he may be convicted even if it is proved, not by any hard evidence but only on circumstantial evidence, that the purpose was or appeared to be prejudicial to the safety or interests of the state.

Section 9 deals with the attempt or incitement of commission of the offences under the Act. This means that even if a person has not committed these offences under the Act, he may still be convicted for attempt or incitement. And punishment for mere attempt or incitement is similar to that for actually committing the offence.

The implications of this vague definition of offences under the OS Act have been aptly pointed out by Chanchal Sarkar in his book *Challenges and Stagnation*. Sarkar says, 'The language of the OSA is wide enough to make it a criminal offence for a messenger at the Home Office to inform a reporter that the Under Secretary is in the habit of taking six lumps of sugar in his tea…'

Section 120-B of the IPC relates to criminal conspiracy to commit an offence. The definition of criminal conspiracy has been provided in Section 120-A. It says, 'When two or more persons agree to do or cause to be done an illegal act, or an act which is not illegal, by illegal means, such an agreement is designated a criminal conspiracy.' By its very definition, criminal conspiracy requires two or more persons' agreement to do an illegal act. In my case I was the only accused. There was not even a mention of an accomplice.

Section 292 of the IPC in the charge sheet relates to pornography. The charge was made more than a month after the registration of the case, based on some spam e-mail and planted VCDs. The complaint made by the Income Tax Deputy Director Saurabh Kumar on 9 June 2002 does not mention recovery of the VCDs. The alleged VCDs were eleven in number. The other basis for slapping of charges under the Anti-Pornography laws were a few spam mails which were sent to my e-mail account. Anybody familiar with the Internet knows that spamming is a worldwide menace. Since my e-mail ID was the official ID for the Delhi Bureau of the *Kashmir Times*, it appears in its printline every day, and was available to the public. I fail to understand the need to accuse me of this, a bailable offence, when a long stay behind bars was ensured by arresting me under the OS Act.

The People's Union for Democratic Rights (PUDR) brought out a report entitled 'Freedom Fettered' on my detention. The report analysed the police rationale: 'The charge of obscenity puts a question mark on Gilani's moral credibility as a person, by trying to show that the Kashmiri Muslim, who is "anti-national," is also "morally depraved"—he not only watches pornography; he invites and incites others into decadence.'

The main basis of the charge of espionage under the OS Act was the recovery of a document from my computer. As I have mentioned earlier, the document was actually annexures of a research paper downloaded from the website of the Institute of Strategic Studies, Islamabad, Pakistan. The complete document had been published by the Institute in 1996 in the form of a booklet as well. The booklet was available with various government and university libraries. The annexures were also sourced to a Paris-based conglomeration of almost 115 human rights group, La Federation Internationale des Droits de l' Homme (FIDH).

The IB officials also planted this document on my father-in-law, Syed Ali Shah Geelani, and tried to prove some kind of nexus between us. They got a case registered in Kashmir as well, and tried to make a case that there was evidence to show that I was the one receiving such 'inputs' from the Valley and then passing them on to identified intelligence operatives in the Pakistan High Commission in New Delhi.

The opinion of the DGMO stated:

(a) *Nature of Document*

(i)   The document is a detailed ORBAT (order of battle) of Army, Rashtriya Rifles and Para Military Forces deployed in Northern Command (J&K). In specific terms, it gives the location, state and strength of Army formations and units deployed in J&K, alongwith the broad areas of deployment of Rashtriya Rifles and Para Military Force battalions.

(ii)   It is definitely not a document originated by the Army. It however appears to contain information compiled by an

agent specifically tasked to observe and report the strength
and location of troops.

(b) *Security value of the Document*. The information contained
in the document is prejudicial to the security of the
country and has serious ramifications on our operational
plans in J&K.

(c) *Utility of Information to an Enemy Country*. The information
in the document is directly useful to our adversary.

(d) *Relationship of document to Defence of the Country*. The
information contained in the document is directly related
to the defence matters of our country.

The police also produced a disclosure memo. According to
this memo, I told them that the Hurriyat Conference leader Syed
Ali Shah Geelani was so impressed with my belief that the Kashmir
problem could not be solved without the involvement of Pakistan
that he married his daughter to me; that an ISI agent met me in
July 1997 in Srinagar and offered me big money to supply
information regarding the deployment of security forces in
Jammu and Kashmir; and that I was collecting information on
the deployment of security forces to pass on to the ISI.

After they received the published version of the allegedly
incriminating document they came up with a supplementary
disclosure memo. The memo again imputed a totally false
statement to me. It said that I had collected information contained
in the document by visiting various offices in the garb of a
reporter and handed over this information to various ISI agents
who visited me, and that the Pakistan government had prepared
the document on the basis of information supplied by me.

The Income Tax officials, who were shown to be the
complainant in the case, had stated that the file on my computer

was created on 17 October 2001. According to the disclosure memo prepared by the police, I came in contact with an agent of the ISI in 1997 at Srinagar and collected and supplied the information afterwards. It also said that the Pakistan government published this document in 1995 on the basis of information supplied by me, though the file in my computer was created only in 2001!

The charge sheet attached a photocopy of my telephone diary to show that I had close connections with the Pakistan High Commission. Is it so unusual for a correspondent of two esteemed Pakistani newspapers, the *Friday Times* and *Daily Times*, a respectable and largely circulated newspaper from Kashmir, the *Kashmir Times*, and Radio Deutsche Welle to have the telephone numbers of the Press Section of the Pakistan High Commission? I did not have a 'close connection' with the high commission, but yes, I did have professional contact, which was perfectly legitimate.

The charge sheet had also attached my e-mail to the deputy executive editor of the *Nation* informing him about arrangements for his stay at the Mughal Sheraton, Agra during the visit of Pakistani President General Parvez Musharraf, as proof of my Pakistani connections.

Details of the bank accounts and other financial transactions related to me and my wife were attached with the charge sheet. There was nothing abnormal in them. All my earnings were above board. Despite what they alleged in the charge sheet, the amount found at my residence during the search was just 3450 rupees.

Interestingly, the prosecution had also produced in the court details of some bank accounts saying that these were my accounts. When I saw them, I immediately demanded an investigation of the said accounts. At that, these allegations vanished into thin air.

The bank account no. 3348416 was in the name of one Rumaisa Geelani in Standard Chartered Grindlays bank, Connaught Place, having a balance of 15 million rupees, and account no. 29224202 in the Development Credit Bank, Connaught Place, in the name of one Imtiyaz Geelani having a balance of 14 million rupees. They also produced some fake ownership papers of a flat in Vasant Kunj in my name.

These details were not filed with the charge sheet. But they were circulated among journalists even after my release, claiming that the IB had found fresh evidence against me. They promised that my freedom was going to be short-lived.

The charge sheet alleged that I had enjoyed the hospitality of the Pakistani government during President Musharraf's visit to Agra. The statement of the lobby manager of the Hotel Mughal Sheraton, attached with the charge sheet, itself negated the contention. The lobby manager said that payment for the room was made by Dost Mohammad Yusufi, India-based special correspondent of the Associated Press of Pakistan (APP). Actually I had not even stayed with Yusufi.

I had gone to Agra to cover the summit meeting between Prime Minister Atal Bihari Vajpayee and President Parvez Musharraf. Ved Bhasin, chairman of the *Kashmir Times* Trust, had also reached there as he had been invited to attend the now-famous breakfast with President Musharraf. Arrangements for his stay were made by the ministry of external affairs, India. I was supposed to stay with him, in the room booked for the *Kashmir Times*.

Though President Musharraf's visit was planned for two days, the summit talks were planned for one day only. The next day President Musharraf was to have breakfast with the editors of leading newspapers and thereafter leave for Ajmer. Therefore day one of the summit was most important for journalists and correspondents. I arrived at the Hotel Mughal Sheraton, where most of the media, both Indian and Pakistani, were staying. A media centre had also been established there.

But the summit did not proceed as planned. A statement made by Sushma Swaraj, union minister of information and broadcasting, created a stir in the Pakistani camp. The Pakistani delegation was supposed to react to the statement. Deliberations went on till late in the night and the Pakistanis came up with a response only at around 2.00 a.m. By the time I filed my story for the *Kashmir Times* it was 4.00 a.m. Yusufi suggested that I stay in his room at the hotel itself as President Musharraf was hosting a breakfast for the editors in the morning and I could get comments of the participating editors. We did not known then that the meeting would be telecast.

Since it was very late, I did not think it proper to disturb Ved Bhasin. So I accompanied Yusufi and stayed with him for the next three or four hours. In the meantime, a hotel staff noted down my name and that was it. I busied myself with work for the next day.

Can this be termed 'enjoying the hospitality of Pakistani government'?

The prosecution scanned more than 10,000 e-mails in their effort to find some evidence that could be used to bolster an otherwise lacklustre case.

The prosecution had alleged that I was in favour of the liberation of Kashmir. To support the contention, besides producing disclosure memos, it also appended an e-mail received by me. On the basis of this e-mail it was alleged that I was collecting information about the Pakistani nationals killed by the security forces in Kashmir.

The e-mail had been sent by Abdul Hamid Khan, chairman of the Balwaristan Liberation Front, and was in fact a copy of the memorandum submitted to the United Nations Commission for Human Rights. Giving details of the human rights situation in Gilgit area of Pakistan-administered Kashmir, the memorandum read:

I would like to draw the attention of this forum towards the fast deteriorating human rights situation. Our nation is under the stifling control of the armed forces of Pakistan and its notorious intelligence agency ISI. Our innocent people are being treated as subjugated slaves. They have been deprived of all basic human, cultural, economical, religious and political rights for the last 52 years. As a result our simple and innocent people are treated worse than animals...

Pakistani administration and its infamous intelligence agency, the ISI, have been forcibly and treacherously sending innocent unemployed youth across the LoC to Indian occupied Kashmir for terrorism and religious cleansing.

The memorandum gave the names and addresses of twenty-seven such youth who had been sent across the LoC by the ISI and were killed by Indian security forces during 1998/99. Besides, the memorandum gave the names of nine persons who 'refused to cross line of control to Indian occupied Kashmir, were picked up and killed by ISI and its mouthpiece Jamaat-e-Islami near the line of control'.

The memorandum appealed 'on behalf of 2 million down trodden people of Balwaristan (Occupied Gilgit Baltistan)' that the former Pakistani President Rafiq Tarar, the then Prime Minister Nawaz Sharif, Army Chief General Parvez Musharraf, General Ziauddin, and the then ISI Chief, General Mohammad Aziz, be brought to the International Court of Justice as 'war criminals'.

By no stretch of imagination can the e-mail and attached memorandum quoted above be considered reflective of my predilections. Nor could it be said that I was compiling names of the Pakistani nationals killed by the Indian security forces in Kashmir. Still, the e-mail was admitted by the court as evidence against me to deny my release on bail.

The illegalities and misrepresentations are apparent in the order issued on behalf of the President by B.R. Dhiman, Under Secretary (Internal Security), ministry of home affairs, Government of India, on 5 September 2002, which states:

> Whereas it is alleged that accused Syed Iftikhar Gilani entered into a conspiracy for collection and communication of information and documents concerning the defence and other matters which was calculated to be or was intended to be or might be useful to the enemy and/or *the disclosure* of which, to an unauthorized person, was prejudicial to the safety, security and interest of the state...

> ...the Central Government *after carefully examining the facts and material before it in regard to the said allegation and circumstances of the case* are satisfied that the said person be tried in a Court of Law for the aforesaid offences punishable under section 3/9 of the Official Secrets Act, 1923 r/w 120 of the IPC and other cognate offences... (Emphasis added.)

The basic premise of the order was factually incorrect. The order said that 'disclosure' of the information and documents was prejudicial to the safety and security of the state. Since the information contained in the document recovered from me was already public, the question of 'disclosing' the same does not arise. One cannot disclose information which is not secret.

The order authorized Ashok Chand, deputy commissioner of police, Special Cell, New Delhi to lodge a complaint under the OS Act, 1923 before the court of competent jurisdiction.

DCP Ashok Chand filed the official complaint under the OS Act on 6 September 2002.

The official complaint filed by DCP Chand was itself a proof of my innocence. Referring to the photocopy of the published version of the annexures of the paper entitled 'Denial of Freedom and Human Rights: A Review of Indian Repression in Kashmir', Paragraph 8 of the complaint said, 'The photocopies of six-paged document were compared and found to be identical with the documents seized during the investigation and the information in the document is identical with the information contained in the five-paged file titled "FORCES" found in the computer of Syed Iftikhar Gilani by the Income Tax Officials on the basis of which the present case was registered.'

■

During my seven-month-long incarceration in Tihar Jail I came across many victims of the Official Secrets Act. The tendency to book people in and around Delhi under the OS Act has assumed menacing proportions particularly over the past three years.

At the time of my arrest, at least thirty other persons were lodged in various jails of Tihar under the OS Act. All the cases pertain to the period 1999–2002. Earlier the OS Act was not so frequently used but after the 13 December attack on Parliament, there is an unusual surge in the number of cases.

Defence Minister George Fernandes stunned the Lok Sabha when he revealed that as many as forty-six serving army personnel and seventeen former army personnel have been jailed for their connections with ISI agents during the last three years.

He added that disciplinary proceedings had been completed against three individuals; one individual was absconding and cases regarding four others were being investigated by the police.

A year ago, Commander Raj Kumar, an accused in a spy case, committed suicide in a jail in Andhra Pradesh. Kumar (52), who was working as chief security officer in the naval armament depot of the Eastern Naval Command, was nabbed by the IB for allegedly associating with an ISI agent, Rajbeer Singh. Kumar hanged himself from the iron rod in the jail's toilet after his bail pleas were rejected.

The Samba spy case had rocked the country in the mid 1970s, when the Military Intelligence arrested fifty-two army personnel for allegedly spying for Pakistan. Two years ago the Delhi High Court gave a clean chit to the two officers who were convicted by the army after court martial proceedings. However the Supreme Court later stayed the Delhi High Court order following an appeal by the government and the hearing is still not over.

Hussamuddin, a carpenter with the army, had a scuffle with an IB official while boarding a bus in Delhi. He was taken to an interrogation centre and made to write names and locations of units where he was posted. Hussamuddin was released recently on bail after spending six years in prison. Mohammad Israr, a clerk, is a co-accused with him. Both of them were arrested in 1991. The case is still hanging in the court.

The case of an Air Force officer, K.C. Saini, makes interesting reading. He was booked for two separate OSA offences but released on bail within months in both while his co-accused, Balram, a sepoy with the Defence Research Development Organisation (DRDO), was in jail for allegedly stealing a computer floppy containing details of T-72 tanks.

Despite the government telling Parliament that there were no leads to suggest that they were supposed to hand over the floppy to agents in the Pakistan High Commission, Balram's bail plea was rejected by both the CMM and the Sessions Court. After spending eleven months in jail, Balram was granted bail by the high court.

Saini had been arrested earlier too by the Central Bureau of Investigation, when it claimed to have busted a spy ring led by Rtd. Air Vice Marshal J.S. Kumar. The matter was hushed up and Saini was released on bail after three months. But he was again picked up in another espionage case by another agency, this time by the Special Cell of the Delhi Police.

Saini claims his crime was that he had reeled out names of private companies dealing with Air Force supplies to whom he had been selling and also named his accomplices in the Purchase Department.

Mohammad Islam, a retired employee of the Border Roads Organisation, was arrested in January 2002 from his home at Deoband in Saharanpur district, Uttar Pradesh, on the basis of an alleged disclosure by one Haji Samiuddin picked up from Dariyaganj area of Delhi. He was allegedly in possession of a map of the Jawahar Tunnel located on National Highway No. 1 between Jammu and Srinagar. According to the charge sheet filed against Mohammad Islam, the 'secret document' found with him was a promotional brochure of the Bharat Heavy Electricals Ltd.

Wasi Akhtar Zaidi, an official with Local Intelligence Unit of Uttar Pradesh Police, is another example of the senseless application of the OS Act. Zaidi claims that the 13 December attack on Parliament was used as an opportunity by IB sleuths who had some problems with him. He was illegally picked up

and taken to the Red Fort, where he was tortured for a week.
They allegedly planted a hand-drawn map of the Meerut
Cantonment and a restricted order signed by former Army Chief
V.N. Sharma on him. Zaidi says he had not even seen the
documents.

Another accused under the OS Act, Mohammad Aslam, an
autorickshaw driver, has been described by the police as a 'petty
smuggler'. He has been accused of passing on sketches of Delhi
and Agra Cantonments as well as details of units located at Meerut
and Roorkee and some amateur photographs of 'vital installations'
like the Delhi Secretariat, the Okhla Barrage and Indian Oil
Corporation.

Ritu Sarin of the *Indian Express* carried out investigations
into the nature of cases pending under the OS Act in various
Delhi courts. Her four-part report in the *Indian Express* from 9
March 2003 to 12 March 2003 is an eye-opener. Sarin wrote,
'Meerut must be India's most sensitive spot. Over the last year
or so, OSA watchers have noticed a strange phenomenon in the
police files. In as many as six cases hand-drawn sketches of Army
cantonments have been produced as evidence against the accused.
And, almost identical sketches of the Meerut Cantonment have
shown up in three cases and unit formations, again at Meerut,
in a fourth. Some lawyers have copied out these sketches on
scrutiny of the evidence.'

In today's world where detailed maps prepared through
satellites are available, does it not seem absurd for any country
to use the services of some novices who can only draw out-of-
scale sketches of some area with fewer details than a tourist map?

Even a senior scientist like S. Nambinarayanan, from the
Indian Space Research Organisation (ISRO), has suffered
imprisonment and mental torture due to the misuse, or

uninformed application, of the OS Act. The National Human Rights Commission has ordered the Kerala government to pay him one million rupees as compensation for trampling upon his human rights.

Summarizing the investigative series on the Official Secrets Act, the *Indian Express* in its editorial of 12 March 2003 said that bizarre arrests under this law do no credit to Indian democracy. The editorial said, 'There is no excuse for the Official Secrets Act to exist in this age of information. The government that enacted the Freedom of Information law and acknowledged its mistake in holding Iftikar Geelani [sic], must now initiate a course correction.'

All conscientious citizens of the country are waiting for this course correction by the government.